# CURRENTS
# OF CHANGE

# CURRENTS
# OF CHANGE

*American Buddhist Women Speak Out
on Jōdo Shinshū*

## PATRICIA KANAYA USUKI

**IBS MONOGRAPH SERIES**     BUDDHIST EDUCATION CENTER

Published by the Institute of Buddhist Studies
Monograph Series and
Orange County Buddhist Church
Buddhist Education Center

Book Design by Arlene Kato

ISBN 978-1-4243-2839-0

Printed in Korea
January 2007
First Edition

The Institute of Buddhist Studies
Monograph Series, Number 2
2140 Durant Street
Berkeley, California 94704

*To all beings heard*
*and unheard.*

# CONTENTS

# EDITORS' PREFACE

W hen people from Japan began migrating to America during the late nineteenth century in search of work and a better life, they carried with them dreams and a willingness to endure the vagaries of a strange land. They also discovered the need for a world both spiritual and social in nature, capable of giving reassurance and empowerment to the dispossessed. Most of those Japanese immigrants were Buddhists, and the tradition that they re-encountered in the new world was Jōdo Shinshū.

Today, Jōdo Shinshū in America finds itself faced with the task of re-identifying itself as an American Shin Buddhist sangha within a broader social, cultural and religious arena. Forces of acculturation, assimilation and an influx of new adherents are working to create a sangha that is increasingly fragmented in its makeup and worldview. These currents of change, it might be said, are pushing Jōdo Shinshū in America in a direction away from its traditional ethnic roots toward a situation that calls for a sangha that is more egalitarian, pragmatic and inclusive of all persons regardless of gender, ethnicity, age or lifestyle,

In this bold and exhaustive examination of Jōdo Shinshū women in America, Patricia Kanaya Usuki addresses the dynamics of change within the Buddhist Churches of America. She begins by explaining the role and treatment of women in the history of the Buddhist tradition, and then engages in a thorough review of developments in the areas of women's studies and sociological perspectives on the assimilation and acculturation of immigrant communities. Based on that context, Usuki then seeks to discover the voices and views of American Buddhist women. Through surveys and interviews, she discovers that women, and some men, of all ages are aware of the stark contrast between the egalitarian teaching of their school and the male-dominant, culturally Japanese institution that continues to exist today.

She concludes, along with many of those interviewed, that the focus of the Jōdo Shinshū sangha must not only "turn from ethnicity to religion in order to remain viable, but that the institution must also make the teaching relevant, understandable, and vibrant to all followers, young and old, male and female, ethnic and non-ethnic." The challenge facing Jōdo Shinshū in America, she offers, can also be viewed as "an opportunity to reinterpret the Shin Buddhist doctrine in new ways that speak to contemporary people everywhere."

The Institute of Buddhist Studies is very pleased to be bringing out this work as the second number in our Monograph Series. The IBS Monograph Series was originally established with the publication of Alfred Bloom's *Life of Shinran* in the early 1990s. The intervening years have produced a variety of difficult challenges for the Institute. Perhaps the most difficult of these was the problem of an adequate facility. Although not suffering any significant damage as a result of the 1989 Loma Prieta earthquake, examination of the seismic integrity of our previous building revealed structural problems that would have been very costly to correct.

In what was supposed to be a temporary relocation, the IBS moved to the grounds of the Mountain View Buddhist Temple. We would like to express our deep appreciation to the membership of that temple, especially as what we had thought would be a two or three year residency stretched out to eight or nine.

Now, the Buddhist Churches of America have established a new Jōdo Shinshū Center in Berkeley that will provide the Institute of Buddhist Studies with a new home for its educational activities. At the same time, under the revitalizing guidance of Bishop Koshin Ogui, the Institute is taking on new challenges—no longer in terms of facilities, but rather in its programmatic offerings.

It is all the more appropriate, therefore, that we now reinvigorate the IBS Monograph Series with the publication of this very important work by Rev. Patricia Kanaya Usuki. We thank Rev. Usuki for allowing the Institute of Buddhist Studies to publish her important and timely work under the title *Currents of Change: American Buddhist Women Speak Out on Jōdo Shinshū*. We are quite sure that women and men, as well as persons of all backgrounds and interests, will find encouragement and inspiration in her clear and vibrant exposition.

Also deserving of our thanks are Bishop Koshin Ogui and Dr. Gordon Bermant for their encouragement that IBS take a leading role in providing these kinds of materials, materials that contribute to the BCA's goal of growing the tradition of Shin Buddhism in the West.

Sincere appreciation is also extended to all those who have made the publication of Rev. Usuki's work possible. Thanks are given to Natalie Fisk for her tireless efforts in the proofing and editing of this text. Finally, we would like to offer heartfelt gratitude to the Buddhist Churches of America Research and Propagation Program, the George Aratani Endowment for the IBS Center for Contemporary Shin Buddhist Studies, the Orange County Buddhist Church Buddhist Education Program, the family of the late Reverend Shobo Ohata, Yukiko and Eugene Otake, and the Berkeley Buddhist Women's Association for their generous financial support of this project.

Gassho,
Richard K. Payne, Ph.D.
Dean of the Institute of Buddhist Studies
Editor-in-Chief of the IBS Monograph Series

David Matsumoto, Monograph Editor
Institute of Buddhist Studies
Center for Contemporary Shin Buddhist Studies

# AUTHOR'S PREFACE

When I was a little girl growing up in Toronto, I would accompany my maternal grandmother to the temple from time to time. I loved being with her, but the services seemed interminable as the minister droned on in a language that was totally incomprehensible to me. I would perk up each time I heard the nembutsu because the final intonation would signal the end of the service, and we could leave.

The temple also meant bazaars, talent shows, and Japanese food cooked by the *fujinkai*. My grandmother was an active member of this women's organization and enjoyed socializing with the other ladies. Outside of the family and work, this was her world, where she could be comfortable speaking and being Japanese. She came from a very devout Shin Buddhist family in the Hiroshima countryside, as did many of the other Issei immigrants.

Though my mother was raised in the Jōdo Shinshū tradition, neither she nor my Nisei father were outwardly religious. My father was raised Anglican in Canada, despite the fact that his clan in Oita Prefecture was and still is Shinshū, and a relative presides over a Nishi Hongwanji temple in my grandfather's hometown. My parents wisely believed that religion was a very personal experience. Sending me to the nearest place of worship, a United Church, to get a grounding in religion, they encouraged me to ask questions and to seek my own path in the spiritual life.

Adulthood brought me to the study of Buddhism and finally, to Jōdo Shinshū. By then conversant in Japanese, I was helped by many teachers in the Hokuriku area – Rennyo's country – to deepen my understanding and my practice. It seems almost ironic that despite my childhood exposure to it, I first came to actually hear the teaching of Shinran in Japan, but the more I studied it, the more I knew that I had found my path.

Experience is a much more effective teacher than words, but there are nonetheless limitations when one is hampered by language shortcomings. Thankfully, Nishi Hongwanji has an International Department that has produced excellent translations of Shinran's works and other texts. I was even more privileged to be able to work in that department and avail myself of the kind tutelage of many learned teachers, as well as attend daily services, dharma talks and frequent seminars. Following my seminary training at Chūō Bukkyō Gakuin in Kyoto and ordination as a minister, I was enabled to complete the Master's program at the Graduate Theological Union in Berkeley, California, to which the Institute of Buddhist Studies is affiliated. Along the way, it was of inestimable assistance to be guided to other bilingual teachers and further translations of scriptures and texts. The number of English language resources on Shin Buddhism is slowly growing, but their relative paucity emphasizes the wonder of any Anglophone being able to follow this rare and incomparable path at all.

Having now been assigned to a temple ministry, I am cognizant of the long road I have traveled to arrive back at a place to which my grandmother first introduced me. However, I also realize that it was the unique combination of causes and conditions in my life that allowed me to meet Shinran and Buddhism as I did. My grandparents' emigration from Japan permitted me to be raised in an environment in which all possibilities are open to all people, without discrimination. I am grateful for an excellent education, as well as unlimited professional opportunities in my first career. These factors, among others, gave me a sense of empowerment and the independence and freedom to break away from convention to search for a deeper meaning in life.

However, I am also aware of the influence that my parents and their parents had on me to make good use of the positive and beneficial conditions I enjoyed and, if I could, to give back to the community that made all of this possible.

Looking at my own childhood temple experiences, I began to wonder how much the atmosphere and attitudes of this particular community had changed, especially for women. Are the teachings more accessible to American-born members than they were several decades ago? Based on what I had learned in Japan, are these teachings still relevant to American women today? While living in Kyoto, I was able to accept that the culture and social thinking were still largely patriarchal, but expected a difference in America. Yet hearing the opinions of certain influential ministers and laymen gave me pause. Did they truly reflect how women currently related to the temple? Informal discussions with women in both the ministry and laity revealed that indeed it would be preferable to find out first-hand. Support for the project was immediate, enthusiastic, and inspiring.

I received much more than I had originally envisaged through the research and writing of this paper. In a truly organic process of information gathering, I began to see a pattern emerging regarding the interrelationship between women, Buddhism, and society. Clearly, we are in an important time of transition not only for American women in Jōdo Shin Buddhism, but also for the contemporary application of Shinran's doctrine itself.

If nothing else, simply having had the honour and the opportunity to record the thoughts of American Shin Buddhist women of all ages, from teens to octogenarians, has been an enriching experience for me not only academically, but also spiritually. To witness to the changing face of the sangha through their experiences is to witness the wonder of the Buddhism in transition and the infinite joy of the dharma in transmission.

I do hope that this work will shed some light on a long-neglected but vital component of Buddhism and its development, so that the past may be reconsidered and the future made whole. As for Jōdo Shinshū in America, it has indeed reached a watershed. The question is, in what direction will the flow be strong and far? Will it continue to trickle on, principally serving an increasingly sparse ethno-cultural group, or will it pick up momentum by adapting itself to the conditions of the environment? Thanks to our social circumstances, women are not only part of the sangha, but they can also be considered to represent the transformation of the sangha so that they are equally qualified to speak for it. Much of what they share in these pages speaks not from their position as women, but as Shin Buddhist followers. In keeping with the principles of Buddhism, this is as it should be, without discrimination. What an exciting time this is for all of us.

It would be impossible to acknowledge all those who have played a role, directly or indirectly, in the shaping and production of this work. When it came time to fulfill the thesis requirement for a Master s degree in Buddhism from the Graduate Theological Union, all of those unnamed but significant entities came together as inspiration for this topic. My gratitude, like the number involved, is beyond measure.

As for the original thesis itself, I am deeply indebted to Rev. David Matsumoto, Dr. Clare Fischer, and Dr. Martin Verhoeven, my thesis committee, for their guidance, encouragement, and scrupulous attention to the development of *Contemporary American Women in J do Shin Buddhism: Tradition, Transition, Transmission* (March 2004), which has now been transformed into this book.

I would also like to extend heartfelt thanks to the many women and youth of the Buddhist Churches of America who participated so enthusiastically in my research, as well as to the Shin Buddhist ministers I interviewed, for their cooperation and support. The work would be meaningless without all of their voices, which deservedly take center stage in these pages.

Special acknowledgment is also due to Rev. Masako Sugimoto of the International Center of J do Shinsh Hongwanji-ha in Kyoto, for her kind assistance, interest, and unflagging patience in tracking down "just one more bit of information."

As noted in the editors preface, it is with the support and efforts, financial and otherwise, of the many organizations and individuals specifically mentioned, that this book has been made possible. I add my utmost expression of gratitude to that of the editors.

Of course, without the Institute of Buddhist Studies and the IBS Center for Contemporary Shin Buddhist Studies in Berkeley, California, the thesis would never have been published. My thanks to all those involved. In particular, I salute Rev. David Matsumoto for seeing the publication through despite the ever-numerous and heavy demands on his time. May I also acknowledge Rev. Marvin Harada and the Orange County Buddhist Church Buddhist Education Center for the role they played in completing this project.

Finally, I would be remiss if I did not express deepest appreciation to Fumiaki Tamon Usuki, my daily sounding-board as husband, fellow minister, and companion on the nembutsu path. Gassho.

January 2007

# INTRODUCTION

The teaching that Śākyamuni Buddha expounded following his enlightenment some 2,500 years ago, known as the Buddha-dharma, is said to be true for all people at all times. Many schools of Buddhism developed from the Buddha's first turning of the dharma wheel and concurrently, various perceptions of women in relation to the dharma came into being through the centuries and across countries and cultures. Though it is said that the Buddha himself proclaimed that women were as capable as men of attaining enlightenment, scriptures written centuries after his demise present contrary views and varied interpretations of the status of women. In Buddhist literature, the portrayal of women as inferior and incapable beings was the norm rather than the exception, and some of what was written even goes so far as to reflect misogynistic attitudes on the part of the author-monks. With few exceptions, we do not know what women themselves had to say about this.

Tracing the transmission of Buddhism from India through China, one cannot ignore the influence of factors such as social attitudes, politics, and economics on the development of the doctrine. However, it is also important to note that the purveyors of Buddhism in turn influenced social attitudes that became prevalent, whether they were supportive of women or not.

Jōdo Shinshū is a form of Mahāyāna Buddhism that was developed in Japan almost 800 years ago by a former Tendai monk named Shinran (1173–1262). Touted by adherents as being a doctrine of universal salvation, we can nonetheless find in its scriptural passages and the writings of its proponents evidence that women were not necessarily regarded as equals, spiritual or otherwise. As regards the institution, officially called Jōdo Shinshū Hongwanji-ha,[1] there is ample evidence that women have not been treated on an equal footing despite the fact that it was Kakushinni, the daughter of Shinran, who first laid the groundwork to keep her father's teaching alive for future generations. Like all forms of Buddhism, the Jōdo Shin doctrine was informed by its era, location, and circumstances. In considering Buddhism in America today, it would be timely to consider whether the teachings of Shinran still speak to women and men, or whether there are elements of the doctrine and its delivery that have outlived their usefulness as skillful means, and may even have negatively affected the way women are viewed within the institution.

The purpose of this study is to examine the views of female practitioners of Jōdo Shinshū in America with regard to the doctrine and the institution of the Buddhist Churches of America (hereafter referred to as the BCA). Is the doctrine still viable to them, and is the institution maximizing on its potential to make it available and relevant to all members? What is the changing role of women in the temples, and what are their objectives?

Throughout Buddhist history, women have played a significant role in the practice and development of its traditions, yet they have been marginalized at best, and most often rendered invisible. Rarely have their writings been preserved, their stories recorded, or their opinions asked. Undoubtedly, the women themselves have been accomplices to their own silence, conditioned by the patriarchal cultures in which Buddhism thrived. Nonetheless, one can piece together enough information from scriptures, historical records, literature, and other writings to realize that social developments had a great influence on women in Buddhism, and that Buddhism in its turn affected the image of women in society. In chapter one, I will demonstrate how this mutual effect took place in ancient India, Sung China, and Kamakura Japan, and how in the process women were able to be active participants in the religion despite the socially inferior status imposed on them. In each instance, the doctrine was as true for them as it was for men, and yet the disjunction between mundane reality and Ultimate Reality was highly evident.

How does the historical link between women, society, and religion relate to Jōdo Shin Buddhism in contemporary America? In chapters three through five, the women speak directly to this issue. Unlike the situation in the past, Buddhist women are now having their voices heard and thoughts recorded. Moreover, it is recognized by some that their input provides essential wholeness to the understanding of a doctrine aimed at all beings. Asking them directly is the only way to get an accurate picture of what they as practitioners of Buddhism feel about their involvement in this religion. It has never sufficed to try to appreciate their experience and aspirations as interpreted and assumed by men, even though this was the accepted practice until only recently. What they share tells much about the relevancy of both the doctrine and the institution in contemporary times, and provides indications of what this may portend for the future of Shin Buddhism everywhere.

The method I used to gather information was through administering surveys and conducting personal interviews. Two surveys were created. The first was for BCA youth, aged fourteen to eighteen, both male and female. I selected this group for analysis because they represent, for the most part, fourth generation members of Japanese descent. Given that sociological studies suggest that this generation is the most acculturated to the American host society, I wanted to investigate whether their views were more egalitarian than those of their forebears, which tended to exhibit influences of a patriarchal society to varying degrees. Surmising that the teenage subjects would reflect American social views of equality, I surveyed males as well as females to test this theory, the results of which are noted further on.

I also surveyed English-speaking female congregants of all generations, who make up a large portion of the mainly ethnic Japanese organization. This survey was widely distributed since I was able to make it available at the national conference of the Federation of Buddhist Women's Associations and subsequently, some members circulated copies further within their temples.

The personal interviews involved women who have demonstrated a breadth of experience in BCA organizational activities, or a commitment to studies in Jōdo Shinshū, or both. I also interviewed female ministers of Shin Buddhism in America to get their perspectives from a teacher's point of view. Since the focus of this investigation was on the perceptions of women with regard to the doctrine and the institution, I did not survey men, though it would be useful to target further research on their views to uncover similarities and contrasts to those of the women.

Responses to the surveys show that the women and youth perceive a great contrast between what they understand as an egalitarian teaching and the male-dominant, Japanese-oriented institution. In other words, women still find the doctrine viable, but they equivocate greatly on the delivery system, arguing that accommodations must be made to make it relevant not only for women, but for everyone inside and outside the ethnic community. Again, the ambient society factors into this because Americans, and this includes Japanese Americans, are more aware than ever before of issues involving equality. It will be seen from the responses to the youth surveys that across the board, the notion of universal equality is fully integrated into their value system. Males as well as females see no reason why there should be any distinction made between the sexes in terms of their function in the temple or elsewhere. Pair this with the women's comments, which indicate that androcentric, patriarchal, and cultural attitudes are a source of frustration both operationally and spiritually, and the urgency to address the situation becomes all the more pressing. Whether prevailing social attitudes will contribute to reshaping this tradition of Buddhism remains to be seen, but if we observe the historical patterns, the potential does exist and this presents exciting possibilities for the development of a contemporary and truly universal form of Jōdo Shinshū.

Indeed, due to the confluence of a number of hitherto unrelated factors, Jōdo Shinshū may actually have arrived at a crucial turning point that could lead it either to stagnation or to unlimited opportunity. The BCA is at a crossroads and must review its raison d'être in keeping with the socio-cultural transformation and the spiritual needs of its current membership. This has been brought to the fore by the phenomenon of acculturation, which affects its members to varying degrees, mostly dependent on generational differences. In addition, because of this acculturation, the third generation Sansei and their offspring have grown up steeped in the atmosphere of American social movements such as equal rights and feminism. Moreover, the uniquely Japanese religious tradition finds itself in a pluralistic society in which it is not uncommon for individuals to question spirituality and religion, and to shop around for a creed that satisfies their personal needs. These days, Americans of all religious backgrounds are undertaking spiritual searches in unprecedented numbers, and increasingly over the past few decades, they have turned their interest to Buddhism.

The typical profile of a new adherent to Buddhism is said to be a well-educated woman from a mainstream religious background, in her forties with an independent source of income[2]. As an indication of new directions in Buddhism, Charles Prebish points out that gender equality is perhaps the foremost trend facing American Buddhism today and quotes Lama Surya Das as saying that "half of the Buddhist teachers in the West are women."[3] Certainly, the list of abbesses, female head teachers, and lay leaders is long and still growing. While this trend is not at all reflected in Shin Buddhism, where only seven out of some sixty active ministers are women, the potential is unquestionably there. In chapter five, women and youth indicate almost unanimous support for women in the ministry and give ample reasons why.

If the number of adherents to American Buddhism is increasing, then why is the membership of the BCA decreasing?[4] It may be that an apparent reluctance to adapt to the acculturation of congregants is driving people away, especially if the focus of the institution is cultural rather than religious. Many of the women stressed that religion had to be the main aim, without which they feel attrition will continue. Associated with this is the fact that not only women's voices, but women's issues have been ignored. Theories relating to acculturation and women in religion are presented in chapter two.

Considering that a large percentage of the membership is composed of women, and that they have a great influence on family participation, their interests are vital to the functioning of the organization. Much of the profile of the newcomer to Buddhism described above could fit many of the BCA's female congregants – but it could also fit those who have left the temple, alienated and dissatisfied. The circumstances of women in Jōdo Shinshū in America are distinctive because of the combination of conditions mentioned earlier. They represent an ethnic Buddhism, yet it is one that has been in this country for five generations. At first glance, it might appear that Shin Buddhist women are subsumed into the traditional Japanese socio-cultural stereotype. Yet it is significant that this form of Japanese Buddhism now finds a locus in the midst of a western society – and congregants – sensitive to equality issues. Thus, for many, the interplay between temple and congregant is different in America than in Japan, but clearly not all interested parties within the institution recognize this. According to the women, there are still ministers and members who maintain influential patriarchal attitudes in the institution, despite the prevailing social environment outside.

These conditions raise a question: Can Jōdo Shinshū in America truly be considered an ethnic Buddhism at all, when the majority of members are English-speaking Americans several generations removed from Japan? Granted, cultural influences continue to give a Japanese countenance to the institution, but how influential is this culture on the everyday lives of the women? Responses indicate that while members respect and value their cultural heritage, many of them see a need to keep it separate from religion. Moreover, they are well aware of the differences in attitude between Japanese and American cultures with regard to women, and it is clear that they view the former as foreign, outmoded, and unrelated to the reality of their lives.

Concurrent with the generational assimilation of ethnic Japanese into mainstream American life, we cannot discount the influence of social developments that have taken place in society in general, particularly during and since the Second World War. These have contributed to a marked difference in lifestyles between second generation Nisei women and their Sansei daughters. Primary among these is a sense of increased independence and a changed self-image resulting from wider access to higher education and employment possibilities. Along with the introduction of the birth control pill, these factors have caused radical change in family roles and family structure that represent a thorough departure from tradition. Interestingly, comments gathered in this research indicate that many Nisei women share the egalitarian views of the younger respondents, even if they appear in the temple to acquiesce to the traditional status quo. For Shin Buddhists in America, the self-effacing and reticent nature of Japanese character carries over to this day in many of its members, and added to this, women have customarily remained in the background. Nonetheless, with five generations to its history, it is not surprising that the demeanor of the Japanese American congregation has changed. In fact, the enthusiastic and grateful response to this investigation in itself suggests that the women are ready and willing to speak out.

Chapter two presents theories that will explain the transformation that is taking place for women in the BCA. One theory discusses the nature of ethnic churches, and a possible paradigm for their evolution in a host society. It posits that the religious institution is regarded as an ethnic enclave for the first generation of immigrants, but that as subsequent generations acculturate, the ethnic focus begins to fade. The institution must then reorient its goals and gradually become more religious and less ethnic if it is to survive. Certainly, this appears to be the underlying tension that is taking place in the BCA, as members grapple with the question of whether their temples are Japanese social and cultural centers, or whether they are primarily institutions for propagating Jōdo Shinshū. In the following chapters, both laywomen and ministers will assert that the goal must be the latter. With respect to the acculturation of Japanese Americans in general, sociologists say that it is complete in everything but appearance, and that the high rate of intermarriage with other races is changing even the visibility factor. On the other hand, studies show that those who are Buddhist tend to be more ethnically oriented – but to what extent? The women who participated in this research are not only homemakers but also salaried workers and professionals in every field of mainstream society. Moreover, further research indicates that third generation Sansei women no longer display the stereotypical attributes of meekness and acquiescence, but are instead more aggressive, assertive, and independent. The surveys and interviews suggest that this description also fits temple women. In the past decade, the number of female temple board presidents and National Council members has steadily increased. Laywomen are also filling a number of other leadership positions at the local, district, and national levels of the BCA. Significantly, contrary to their submissive image, second generation Nisei women also expressed frank criticisms and opinions about the institution, indicating that there has been a need to ask questions of them.

The change in posture relates to the second focus of chapter two, linking feminism to religion. In this section, it is observed that while the basic doctrine of Buddhism may be egalitarian in nature, the delivery and institutionalization of the Buddha-dharma, through its writings and organizational bodies, has been largely androcentric and patriarchal. Since the beginning, Buddhism conformed to social custom, and over time proponents even came to use such conformity to political and financial advantage. Examples of this are documented in chapter one, and show that it was gradually assumed that women were inferior. Shin Buddhism, with its vow to transform women into men and its system of patrilineal inheritance, is no exception.

Because of the bias, it is important to consider and develop a female perspective both to serve the whole sangha[5] more appropriately and to lend balance to the teaching of the dharma for all beings. The shortcoming is all the more noticeable in American society where notions of equal worth and equal access rank among the top social concerns of the day. However, Buddhist institutions everywhere are being pressed to review their attitudes toward women and revalorize traditions, where necessary, to return to the original intent of the doctrine.[6] Indeed, that the core doctrine is not androcentric in nature can be viewed as a great advantage and opportunity for Buddhism.

Parallels are often drawn between feminism and Buddhism, in that both are concerned with definitions of the self; liberation; mental constructs; and experiential verification, albeit from different approaches. It is therefore not surprising that the two are compatible with each other.

Further, researchers stress that if women serve as role models both in lay leadership and in the ministry, they validate female participation in the church and further empower other women. The objective, however, is to end up with a more integral and holistic view within the institution, and not to replace androcentrism with its opposite. Members acknowledge this through their comments, indicating that they are simply looking for a needed balance and an opening up of all possibilities to all people.

Will their insights fall on deaf ears? It is possible that the forces of tradition, entrenched power, and ego will cause the institution to continue to ignore a very important constituency. On the other hand, transformation may take place within the existing institution, due in no small part to the growing participation of women. Indeed, the transition appears to be proceeding as a matter of course, reflecting a general change in the outlook of the membership at large. Several people reported that men are just as supportive of women's initiatives, demonstrating that it is not only the women who have changed with the times.

According to the acculturation theory, if the institution fails to readapt its goals, it will eventually face extinction. Would this spell the end of Jōdo Shinshū in America? On a less dramatic level, if women found that they could not satisfactorily meet their religious needs within the existing institution, what are their alternatives? Based on the experiences of other American Buddhist women, this would not necessarily be the end of the story. Women who see the doctrine as a viable path to spiritual awakening do not need to rely on the established order to realize fulfillment. As women have done for centuries, in Japan and in other countries, they can find their way around the obstacles and focus on the teaching. In the United States, female teachers of other schools of Buddhism are creating new organizational forms and networking with their sisters all over the world to amplify their ability to learn and to serve. Intimations reported in this study indicate that some Shin Buddhist women are prepared to do the same.

We seem to be at a turning point in the history of Jōdo Shinshū and it is taking place here in America. Of course this does not concern women only, but women are both major movers and beneficiaries in the process. In its new American environment, Shin Buddhism is due to be rebalanced and women are naturally positioned to make a significant contribution. The causes and conditions surrounding ethnic women in Shin Buddhism in America place them in a position to make a unique contribution because their history has the potential to inform new developments in the interpretation of Buddhism for contemporary society.

This research shows the importance of giving women a platform to be heard, for their insights and experience are significant to the continuing accessibility of Buddhism. Karma Lekshe Tsomo illustrates the larger picture as follows:

> Reflecting on Buddhist history, we see the recurrent paradigm of populist renewal in response to elitist domination and stagnation[7] … Buddhism undergoes periodic declines and renewals to redeclare its relevance to everyday life. A natural process of synthesis and transformation occurs continuously through the reevaluation and reinterpretation of cultural values, resulting in an ongoing symbiosis of imported and indigenous systems of thought … Once again Buddhism must demonstrate its relevance and effectiveness on a practical level – synthesizing Asian and Western insights and values, ancient and modern. A revaluation of women's place in the tradition and a forum for voicing women's concerns are key elements in the personal and intellectual dynamics of this process.[8]

It appears that Jōdo Shin Buddhist women in America are right on course.

PART ONE

# BUDDHIST WOMEN IN ASIA: A BACKGROUND

# CHAPTER ONE

# WOMEN, SOCIETY, AND BUDDHISM: A HISTORICAL PERSPECTIVE

*The only generalization that can perhaps be made with any validity about the position of woman in Buddhist lands and the role she played and still plays is that neither her position nor her role was ever negligible or trifling.*

I.B. Horner[1]

While it is impossible to document some 2,500 years of the history of women in Buddhism in this short chapter, it would be useful to trace some recurring themes that have followed women's participation in the religion through the centuries and across cultures. These themes do not entail religion or doctrine alone, but spotlight the social, cultural, political, and economic variables that determined the nature of women's participation as practitioners of Buddhism. Indeed, it is necessary to consider these elements in the development of both the doctrine and the institution of Buddhism as it grew from the early days of Gautama Buddha's sangha in India and traveled eastward through China and other Asian countries including Japan. The focus of this research is on women in Jōdo Shinshū in contemporary America, and these variables have been no less influential in determining the role women are playing in the institution today.

In this chapter, I will demonstrate how women have been instrumental in the development of Buddhist doctrine and of the institution, focusing primarily on three distinct epochs as examples of the interplay between society and religion. The study begins with an examination of the role of women in early Indian Buddhism. It then leaps forward about a millennium to Sung China and the mutual transformations that took place between women and Buddhism at that time. Finally, I will focus on Buddhist women in thirteenth century Kamakura Japan when Jōdo

Shinshū and other new schools of Japanese Buddhism first saw light. Though each epoch represents a very different time, place, and culture, it becomes evident that the role of women surpasses the passive one that society or the institution may have wished to impose on them.

Before turning to the specific eras, I would like to comment on the portrayal of women in Buddhist scriptures throughout its history. It is apparent from the beginning that doctrine affected society and that social and cultural values in turn affected the institutions and therefore doctrinal developments in an arguably endless cycle. Thus, though the basic tenets of Buddhism have remained unchanged, the means by which they have been conveyed have been a reflection of each society and era through which Buddhism has passed. Considering this, no picture of Buddhism would be complete without taking into account the daily lives of its adherents. Moreover, to do so is to impart a critical balance to the portrayal of women, given the fact that the Buddhist scriptures and almost all writings about Buddhism until the modern era were written by men, many of whom were monastics with particular religious agendas. What they wrote about women did not necessarily reflect reality on either plane, whether mundane or transcendent. Rather, as Diana Paul puts it,

> [In a patriarchal power structure] the feminine is frequently associated with the secular, powerless, profane, and imperfect. Male Buddhists, like male religious leaders in other cultures, established normative behavior for women by creating certain ideals of femininity.[2]

Paul, in her analysis of nineteen episodes from Mahāyāna scriptures, finds two central cross-cultural themes in the texts. One is a dualistic view, portraying the female as sensual, destructive, and polluting; an entity to be suppressed and controlled by the male. As such, women are relegated to the margins of society and religion. The other is an integrative view, portraying the female as wise, maternal, creative, and compassionate.[3] Alan Sponberg agrees that not one monolithic Buddhist view of women, but four distinct attitudes are represented in the scriptures, which he names soteriological inclusiveness; institutional androcentrism; ascetic misogyny; and soteriological androgyny.[4] These classifications are useful for explaining how women were viewed scripturally, but I would argue that not all practices fit neatly into one category or another. For example, though Sponberg refers to certain *Vinaya* texts when speaking of institutional androcentrism, he does not address the fact that institutional androcentrism is pervasive as a practice, regardless of the kind of scriptures Buddhist institutions propound. In addition, some doctrines seem to defy his classification scheme, such as the need for women to change to male form in order to attain Buddhahood. Since this is alluded to in the main scripture of Jōdo Shinshū, I will analyze the phenomenon in more detail in the section on Kamakura Buddhism and Shinran's view of women.

## WOMEN IN INDIAN BUDDHISM

Scholars such as Diana Paul, Susan Murcott, and Nancy Falk base their studies on literature and scriptures.[5] They tend to offer a subjective interpretation of how women were actually regarded in the preliminary years of Buddhism. Others, such as Richard Gombrich, take into account prevailing social, economic, and political trends.[6] I.B. Horner, whose groundbreaking work in 1930 on early Buddhist women is still foundational, chooses to fit the social context into the religious.[7] Still others, like Buddhist activist Karma Lekshe Tsomo and feminist Rita Gross use modern rationales to explain the apparent contradiction between the dharma and the inequitable treatment of the women.[8]

It is significant that the few extant Buddhist works said to have been written by women were set down by early Buddhist nuns in India. These are the poems of the *Therīgāthā*, as well as the *Bhikkhuni Samyutta* and parts of the *Apadāna*. However, it must be remembered that in the time of the historical Buddha, Śākyamuni, "the position of women in Buddhist India was more enviable and more honourable than it had been in pre-Buddhist days… [women] commanded more respect and ranked as individuals. They enjoyed more independence, and a wider liberty to guide and follow their own lives."[9] Jonathan Walters and others concur that women wielded more power at the time of the Buddha than at any time before or after this epoch.[10] The social climate of the day was remarkably suggestive of present-day conditions. India was enjoying an era of economic strength in which organized trade, new transportation infrastructures, and technological advances were literally reshaping the landscape. Urbanization developed, along with an important merchant class, and there was a move away from centralized kinship communities to larger, impersonal social structures. This meant greater independence, freedom, and mobility for both men and women, especially at higher social levels where wealth and status offered choices. With more free time and increased social awareness, people began to focus on civil rights and higher ethical ideals, leading to a refreshed interest in religion and philosophy. As the social structure was transformed, so too were the corresponding ideologies. Sponberg suggests that the rise of Buddhism was concurrent with "a new sense of self-consciousness or individuality, especially for those who were on the margins, socially or spiritually,"[11] and others posit that there was an enhanced appreciation and cultivation of female spirituality.[12] Certainly, Buddhism appealed to all kinds of people for its non-discriminatory egalitarianism and its rejection of superiority based on birth.

Nonetheless, unlike men, women of the day were constrained to fulfill their social obligations to family before turning their efforts to spiritual pursuits, for there was a distinct separation of the sacred and the profane in the lives of people. As with Siddhārtha himself, it was socially acceptable for men to relinquish responsibilities to family and home to become religious renunciants. For women, however, the demands of motherhood and the home took precedence and they had no time to explore the spiritual path until free of these duties. The very nature of their role affected both the perception of women and the ways in which various schools of Buddhism eventually came to allow for their spiritual salvation. Yet in reality, there was no question of women having a lower capacity for spiritual attainment, as was suggested in scriptural writings penned by monks centuries later. It was simply that women were not free to do as they wished.

In this environment, Buddhism could nonetheless take root because it was concerned not with social reform, which would have been disruptive and threatening to the ruling class, but with individual spiritual enlightenment.[13] It is for this reason, then, that early nuns were necessarily those without families, such as widows, prostitutes, and the childless. Moreover, if popular accounts of the first Buddhist nun, Mahāprajāpati (the Buddha's stepmother) are true, a picture emerges of a number of strong and determined women who, despite the Buddha's purported threefold rejection, persisted in hounding him barefoot for over a hundred miles in order to change his mind about allowing women into the sangha.[14] Once the Buddha did allow the creation of a nuns' order, women held prominent places in his company as practitioners and teachers. Not only did he predict and facilitate attainment of enlightenment for specific individuals among them, but he also declared that any woman, nun or lay, was as capable of attaining enlightenment as a man. This illustrates Sponberg's first category of soteriological inclusiveness, meaning that women could attain enlightenment, but were not necessarily equal to men. He notes that while the Buddha's view may have been doctrinally egalitarian, he made no comment on women's rights within society at large.[15] Sponberg's second category of institutional androcentrism is thus also illustrated here, for egalitarian soteriology notwithstanding, the Buddha himself was a product of his society and his perceptions and precepts were influenced accordingly. Therefore, it may have been socially acceptable to all concerned that women in the sangha were still regarded as inferior to men and subjected to extra monastic rules not only for their own protection, but also to protect the reputation of the monks who relied on public financing. Especially after the Buddha's death, scriptures show that the institution became ever more regulated, gradually shifting the focus away from women's spirituality to the integrity of the institution within the larger community.

As Charles Prebish points out, stories of the Buddha's initial rejection of women are legion, while articles and books about the contribution of Buddhist monastic women are not.[16] On the other hand, it is known that many laywomen found some spiritual satisfaction in demonstrating religious devotion by supporting the institution financially. There are numerous recorded instances of almsgiving and donations by laywomen and nuns as a purchasing of merit, both in writings and on epigraphical inscriptions.[17] In fact, women played a key economic role in supporting Buddhism right from the start. Janis Willis writes that the Buddha was patronized by a number of wealthy women, including merchants, prostitutes, and queens.[18] In exchange for this dedication and selflessness, women, including mothers, were normally awarded a certain degree of respect and veneration that gave them recognizable power. Thus, within the domestic sphere, Buddhism provided possibilities for women to be seen in an improved light.

Scripturally too, I.B. Horner interprets the duties of a husband and wife, according to the *Sigala Sutta*, as indicating equality, mutual caring, and respect.[19] Indeed, recognizing that the contents of sutras are meant to be interpreted as skillful means to understanding the import of the dharma, the specific duties may well have been appropriate for the times. Nonetheless, this epoch was no different from many Buddhist cultures even today, in that women were subjected to what were then known as the laws of Manu: dependent on fathers at birth; dependent on husbands upon marriage; and dependent on sons upon widowhood. To this, we might add that nuns were dependent on charity just as their sangha brothers were. In this light, though, references to women in some Buddhist writings appear to indicate a negative view of nuns and a positive view of laywomen. This may have less to do with misogyny as with economics: nuns had nothing, laywomen gave all.[20] Of the latter, Willis asserts that they were "independent and active in the world, and as capable of affecting and, in some cases, even of shaping, the development of the Buddhist tradition."[21]

Then, what of Sponberg's third category, that of ascetic misogyny? Based on available sociological and historical information, it appears that scriptures portraying such a view of women were a reflection of later times, when the political power structure of monks had solidified and the impartial guidance of the Buddha himself was no longer available.[22] Some writings argue that beings are born female as a result of past evil karmic actions that make them inferior morally and spiritually.[23] The Buddha had been convinced to change his mind about allowing women into the sangha because of a logical argument regarding their spiritual ability, which apparently he could not and would not deny despite the prevailing social opposition. His touchstone was the dharma, whereas the same cannot necessarily be said of those who came to use Buddhism and its institution for personal and political purposes.[24] Monks did not need unnecessary competition for power and financing, and giving nuns a negative image for whatever reason also kept them subordinated. To be charitable, it must be acknowledged that the institution was always under pressure to conform to social custom, relying as it did not only on material sustenance, but also on the sanction and support of the state. It would not have been difficult for monks to conform, particularly as they had already renounced personal involvement with women in entering the sangha. Judging by *Vinaya* rules, of which there were many more for nuns than for monks, it appears that there was a recognition of the necessity to maintain strict moral and social standards.

No doubt there were monks whose practice focused on ascetic purity, and fear of the feminine power to undermine their celibacy fomented the vilification of women in scriptures.[25] However, such practices fly in the face not only of soteriological inclusiveness, since women were depicted as being beyond redemption, but also of the necessary Middle Path propounded by the Buddha. Though visualizing the female as inferior, disgusting, and corrupt may have been a common monastic practice, such texts did not embody the primary teachings. Moreover, they did not characterize the practical religion of the people at large, who may even have been unaware of such practices, or could not find relevance to their daily lives. Certainly, there was a distinction between monastic and lay.

Indeed, regarding scriptures, Paul found "an increase in both popularity and influence among Buddhists as the texts became more egalitarian."[26] Here we would find Sponberg's fourth category of soteriological androgyny, which he says did not surface in the scriptures until after the sixth or seventh century (C.E.)[27] Leading up to this, Paul traces a growing acceptance of females as bodhisattvas, teachers, and "good friends," but finds that they are stratified into three categories: denial of entrance into a Buddha land in female form, as in the *Larger (Sukhāvatīvyūha) Sutra's* thirty-fifth vow (to be discussed later) and the *Lotus (Saddharmapundarīka) Sutra's* Naga Princess; acceptance of women as lower stage bodhisattvas, as described in the *Lotus Sutra*; and finally acceptance of women as advanced bodhisattvas and imminent Buddhas, as in the *Vimalakīrti Sutra* (*Vimalakīrti-nirdeśa*) and the *Śrīmālā Sutra* (*Śrīmālādevi*).[28] The last group represents a small percentage of the sutras, but they became very popular and influential Mahāyāna texts that placed an emphasis on the metaphysical state of the "conditioned" and the "unconditioned," essentially expounding non-duality of any kind – hence, no difference between male and female. Sponberg calls this crucial shift in perspective "revalorization of the feminine... reassessment of the soteriological relevance... of socially defined gender characterizations in general, a reevaluation of all those qualities and expectations culturally ascribed to male and female."[29] The classification is different from soteriological inclusiveness, which merely stated that sex and gender were irrelevant to attainment. Where before there was a "lack of a clear conceptual distinction between biological sex and social gender,"[30] a new perspective on the nature of sentient beings was emerging – or re-emerging. Paul notes that the *Agañña Sutta*, an earlier text in the Pali canon that describes the mythological beginnings of the world, portrays an ideal environment of non-duality before male and female came to be. She describes it as "a state of perfection which is asexual, noncorporeal, and beyond notions of good and evil. Physical devolution is concomitant with moral degeneration."[31] Could it be that the concepts of some scriptures, too, were actually devolving as they responded to social values of each "civilization?"

However popular "androgynous" scriptures were, like the earlier misogynistic writings, evidently these did not have a pervasive or lasting impact anywhere in the Mahāyāna world.[32] Perceptions of people in Buddhist societies did not evolve at the same rate of enlightenment, and hierarchies and discrimination continued to flourish within the Mahāyāna Buddhist institution.

## WOMEN IN CHINESE BUDDHISM

Though this study does not concentrate on women in monastic life, as Jōdo Shinshū is not a monastic tradition, it merits mention that the first order of Chinese Buddhist nuns was established in the fourth century C.E. Gradually, participants enjoyed some measure of freedom to study, teach, and even wield influence in affairs of state. Unlike their antecedents in India, women could choose the monastic life as an alternative to marriage. As mentioned earlier, it was during the sixth century that the positive image of women and female bodhisattvas appeared in sutras. Traditional views that women had spiritual limitations were challenged and there was a special interest in such sutras as the *Vimalakīrti* and the *Śrīmālā*. The T'ien-t'ai school taught that all beings had the same potential to attain Buddhahood, and in this very life, as shown by the *Lotus Sutra's* Naga Princess. Empress Wu (625–705 C.E.), influenced by the political and feminist ideas of the *Avatamsaka Sutra,* further interpreted new Mahāyāna attitudes toward women as arguments for the female right to wield power. Proclaiming herself a bodhisattva and *cakravartin*,[33] she made Buddhism the state religion of China.

However, by the early part of the Sung Dynasty (960–1279 C.E.), Buddhism in China was entering its demise as neo-Confucian values began to hold sway. Nonetheless, the Sung was notable for its dynamic growth and transformations socially, politically, and economically, as well as in the sphere of religion. In all of these areas, there arose greater integration between classes. Religion itself displayed a porosity of ideas between Buddhism, Confucianism, Taoism, and the popular indigenous religions. Still, it remained a patriarchal society. In order to understand how women were able to enjoy some measure of independence, again one must look beyond sources such as formal religious and secular histories, biographies and epigraphs that portray men's ideal image of the submissive woman. Fortunately, there are also extant literary narratives by men and women, as well as popular stories and recorded judicial cases that give an expanded idea of how women really lived.[34]

As in ancient India, expanded commerce created a new gentry class. Particularly with the invention of printing, women were able to study philosophy and religion to the extent that their impact came to be significant not only financially, as they consequently supported the establishment of monasteries and institutions, but also doctrinally. By this time, Buddhism had matured as a fully sinicized tradition. Chinese schools such as T'ien-t'ai, Hua-yen, Pure Land and Ch'an (Zen) had developed the attractive idea of universal Buddha nature (*tathāgatagarbha*) and these new schools questioned the division that once existed between the secular and sacred realms. That leaving home was no longer a necessary prerequisite to spiritual salvation was of paramount significance, not only because it increased the involvement of the laity, but also because the home was the center of Chinese life into which Buddhism now entered.

Just as in ancient India, women in Sung China were generally relegated to maintaining the lineage of the household and running the household itself. Thus, they continued to act as obedient daughter, faithful wife or sacrificing mother. Still, such a role permitted women not only to study and practice religion, but also to influence their families. Indeed, the role of the woman as mother afforded her the greatest chance for power and control in her life, particularly with respect to her sons. Alan Cole has devoted an entire study to the subject of the relationship between mothers and sons and Chinese Buddhist doctrine. He claims that the Buddhist institution created "family propaganda" for the purposes of increasing donations toward its monasteries by capitalizing on the idea of filial indebtedness.[35] Women were presented as sinners who were sent to the netherworld to suffer, simply by dint of their femalehood. Only the religious devotion of their offspring would save them. This is illustrated in the famous story of Mu Lian (Skt. Maudgalyāyana, Jp. Mokuren) who liberates his mother from the tortures of hell.[36] Though denigrating to women, such new scriptures afforded them recognition they had not previously enjoyed.[37] It was at this point that Chinese people became convinced of the need to buy merit for the deceased by supporting the religious institution, and it was a significant event for Buddhism because it solidified and defined monastic-family arrangements. Moreover, because adherence to such teachings ensured filial devotion, more women of all classes began to support and participate in the practice of Buddhism.

As for women of the educated upper classes, they were equally interested in the spiritual possibilities that the philosophy of Buddhism presented for them. Despite the neo-Confucian backlash against Buddhism, the Ch'an School came to flourish by emphasizing that the mind of enlightenment was without distinguishing characteristics. Such a teaching led some women into relinquishing the home life to further their spiritual quest, but others studied with nuns while carrying on their domestic responsibilities.

It is known that two key Ch'an teachers of the concept, Ta-hui Tsung-kao (1089–1163 C.E.) and Hung-chih Cheng-chueh (1091–1157 C.E.) taught female disciples and had female dharma heirs, both nuns and laywomen. A nun named Miao-tao was Ta-hui's first dharma heir and as an abbess in many nunneries, became a renowned teacher of women. Her awakening in 1134 C.E. was said to have been critical in Ta-hui's own career and pivotal in the success of his teaching methodology. Eventually, Miao-tao became eminent in her own right, teaching in the Lin-chi (Jp. Rinzai) tradition quite independent from her teacher's style. These developments did much to advance the rhetoric of equality. By the thirteenth century, women could have dharma heirs and enjoyed a status that was exceptional. In addition, the era also produced numerous stories of laywomen of various classes challenging and teaching men and demonstrating equality as awakened beings.

The increased participation of women in both lay and monastic life led to an increase in the attention paid to them by Buddhist institutions. Monks wrote more about women's achievements and began addressing issues of special concern to women. This served the purposes of both supporting the doctrine and ensuring financial contributions from female patrons. That the image of the female was undergoing a positive transformation is demonstrated by the fact that it was during this era that the image of the bodhisattva Guanshiyin (Skt. Avalokiteśvara, Jp. Kannon) changed from male to female.[38]

Chinese society gradually succumbed to stronger patriarchal control, just as it had in India, yet the Sung was a time of growth, change and interchange between classes, between religions, and between sexes. Thus, it was no paradox that portrayals of the female, both real and ideal, could represent such a diversity of images and that not only were these images created by circumstances of the day, but that they in turn also influenced developments in all facets of life. Though we do not have a complete picture of women of the Sung, we can conclude that their collective image, both limited and liberated, represented the multi-dimensional reality of a society and a religion in transition.

# WOMEN IN JAPANESE BUDDHISM

Buddhism was introduced into Japan in the sixth century C.E. from Korea, and by the Nara era (710–781 C.E.) the main doctrines of Chinese Buddhism had been introduced directly from China. The first nuns were ordained in 584 C.E.[39] According to Bernard Faure, nuns performed important roles, equal to those of monks, during the Nara period. However, by the Heian era (794–1185 C.E.), the male-dominated Buddhist institutions had come to prohibit female ordination.[40] It is said that Heian noblewomen found diversion in Buddhist services, ceremonies, and retreats, but by this time, "Japanese Buddhism, tainted by its Chinese parent, offered somewhat less equality than Indian Buddhism."[41] In fact, Faure believes that "the general acceptance of Buddhist prejudices against women after the ninth century was not the result of a general decline in the status of women, but rather one of its causes."[42] Significantly, it was during this period too, that Buddhist institutions began to rely heavily on the patronage of aristocrats and became alienated from the masses.[43]

A turbulent age of social change followed the Heian era as wars raged and feudalism became entrenched. The Kamakura era (1192–1332 C.E.) saw the emergence of the new schools of Japanese Buddhism, including Jōdo Shinshū, a doctrine created by Shinran (1173–1262 C.E.) who referred to himself as "neither priest nor lay."[44] These schools were marked by their teachings of universality, through which all beings were understood to have the ability to attain enlightenment. This meant that the benefits of Buddhism were no longer confined to the courts of the nobility and to the monasteries, but that the religion could be practiced by the masses. Monks who had hitherto been secluded in all-male environments now had to consider female soteriology and view women in a different way. Alicia and Daigan Matsunaga contend that this was the point at which the religion took on a truly Japanese nature in Japan.[45]

Due to the limitations of space, I would like to confine my subsequent comments to social, historical, and doctrinal factors involving women and Jōdo Shinshū, with a view to understanding why the doctrine and the institution display indications of androcentrism to this day.

The essence of Shin Buddhism appears in the *Larger Sutra*, wherein the forty-eight vows of Dharmākara Bodhisattva to become Amida Buddha are made known. Supreme among these vows is the eighteenth, known as the Primal Vow.[46] Simply put, the vow presents the possibility for all beings to attain enlightenment, as there is "no discrimination between noble and humble or black-robed monks and white-clothed laity, no differentiation between man and woman, old and young."[47] Indeed, the content of this vow is by far the most prominently known among Shin Buddhist followers.

However, there is a vow that refers specifically to women. It is known variously as the thirty-fifth vow, "The Aspiration for Rebirth of Women," "The Aspiration to Become a Male," or "The Aspiration to Change from Female to Male."[48] Clearly, the vow does not fall into any of Sponberg's categories. It is inclusive, but only to the extent that women must first change to male form to achieve full enlightenment. I would argue that it is not misogynistic, as some assert, because it is merely recognizing a social fact about being born a woman that appears to have been a constant throughout the period of this historical study. The lot of women was not an enviable one, particularly if they were regarded as inferior. That this was a reflection of social perceptions can be seen in the following version of the same vow, based directly on a Sanskrit text:

> ... If, after I have obtained bodhi, women in immeasurable,
> innumerable... Buddha countries on all sides, after having
> heard my name, should allow carelessness to arise, should
> not turn their thoughts toward Bodhi, should, when they are
> free from birth, not despise their female nature; and if they,
> being born again should assume a second female nature,
> then may I not obtain the highest perfect knowledge.[49]

The later Chinese version used by Shinran (see note 48), translated from Sanskrit by Samghavarman during the Ts'ao-Wei Dynasty (220–265 C.E.), and still used by Shin Buddhists today, might have reflected prevailing attitudes of third century China. Indeed, taking this one step further, we now have a contemporary translation into English from the classical Chinese, the former of which, while bound by certain constraints of the content of the latter, is nonetheless informed by the translator's knowledge of current trends of social thought. Hence, the importance of the key phrase, "who... *wish* to renounce womanhood ..." I will explore contemporary explications of this vow in the next chapter.[50]

To return to the Kamakura era, how did Shinran justify this apparent dichotomy in promoting his doctrine of equality? It must be recognized that the Shin doctrine maintains that a person can attain a faith[51] awakening in his or her current lifetime, and that full enlightenment is then guaranteed upon death. Were this true, why would women necessarily have to change their form before entering the Pure Land? The question is reminiscent of those raised about the Naga Princess in the *Lotus Sutra*, who changes her form to attain the high bodhisattva stage of non-retrogression and then becomes a Buddha.[52] Some apologists maintain that such a deed was meant as a compassionate act of skillful means (*upāya*) to assist men like Śāriputra to prevail over their worldly attachment to differentiation of sex.[53]

Others, like Paul, explain that the transformation was necessary to allow the princess to overcome the five kinds of high status denied to women, known as the Five Obstacles.[54] This and the Three Submissions (subservience to father, husband and son) were developed in India. The latter continued in Chinese society, but the former did not appear to pose any major obstructions for women there.[55] However, Faure maintains that the Buddhist institution was responsible for the spread of these ideas in medieval Japan, as evidenced by Japanese literature of the time.[56] He asserts that significant changes in the perception of women took place by the ninth century and that the Five Obstacles came to be regarded as an outright exclusion from Buddhahood and sacred places such as Mt. Hiei.[57] Later, female vows and prayers thus alluded to the Obstacles, enabling monks simply to classify women with *hinin*, Japan's outcast society. As a result, rather than helping them at least on a mundane level, the institution further exacerbated the negative perception toward women.[58] Thus, by the Kamakura era, even though soteriology was arguably inclusive, the new doctrines did nothing to subvert patriarchal dominance within the institution.

It is important to note that the Buddhist institution not only abetted but also harmonized with escalating social discrimination against women and that in fact many women accepted and internalized the negative views. However, not all women were so passive. Extant poetry suggests that a few women saw the notion of female inferiority as a male fabrication and questioned its consonance with Pure Land doctrine.[59] On the other hand, popular belief held that menstrual defilement could be alleviated by reciting the Pure Land chant of the nembutsu.[60] Thus, by reinforcing female guilt, proponents of the teaching made it attractive to those who were grateful that it encompassed everyone, "even women." Some even see this and other universal vows as the democratization of Buddhism.[61] Practically speaking, if women of the day believed this to be true, it would explain why Jōdo Shinshū and other new schools were so popular. Such a movement would have been beneficial to someone like Shinran who had no institutional backing, and relied on the support of the masses to enable his proselytizing, studies, and survival.

Moreover, Shinran, like Śākyamuni Buddha in his time, was the product of a patriarchal society. At age nine, after his mother died, he was sent to Mt. Hiei, a sacred place forbidden to women, to spend the next twenty years as a Tendai monk. It is possible that he truly believed that women were in need of extra help, as evidenced by this hymn that he wrote:

> If women did not entrust themselves to Amida's Name and vow,
> They would never become free of the five obstructions,
> Even though they passed through myriads of kalpas;
> How, then, would their existence as women be transformed?[62]

Shinran repeatedly wrote and taught that the Primal Vow was meant for all sentient beings without discrimination. That the thirty-fifth vow existed in a sutra written centuries before was not something for which he attempted to apologize.[63] On the contrary, given the social climate of his times, he may well have viewed it as a compassionate concession to those who were less privileged. Certainly, he was not a misogynist. His marriage to a well-educated upper class laywoman, Eshinni (1182–?), though perhaps not a first for a priest, helped to change views of the ability of women and the laity to participate in the spiritual path.

Evidence that Shinran and Eshinni supported and respected each other in the religious pursuit is chronicled in her letters to their youngest daughter, Kakushinni (1224–1283).[64] These letters show that not only was Eshinni refined, intelligent and educated, but also that she was financially independent, owning both property and servants over whom she had complete discretionary authority regarding management and inheritance. Moreover, her letters give a vivid description of the everyday life of a woman in an era troubled by famine and unrest, struggling to feed and clothe herself and her dependents through her own manual labour despite her social class, while Shinran pursued his studies far away in Kyoto. At the same time, her writings confirm her abiding faith in both her husband and his doctrine, demonstrating how her spiritual life was intertwined with the harsh reality of her everyday existence. While most scholars and theologians focus on the import of the letters in terms of the information they convey about Shinran, few have noted their significance for what they tell us about the practical dimension of the doctrine relating to women and their spiritual fulfillment.[65] It must be remembered that Jōdo Shinshū was one of the "new schools" that opened up Buddhism to the masses without discrimination, so here we find chronicled one of the first instances of a laywoman living her life in the teaching and exhorting her daughter to do the same.

In her turn, Kakushinni was driven by devotion not only to her father, but to his research and teaching as well. Using land made available to her by her second husband, she joined with followers after her father's passing to keep his memory and his teachings alive. Until her own demise, she was appointed as caretaker to the memorial shrine they erected on the land. It is known from her extant letters that she bequeathed the gravesite to all Shinshū followers and wished to pass the position of caretaker on to her descendents, subject to the approval of followers. However, it is noteworthy that her husband did not require her to pass the property on to their son.[66] In fact, the blood lineage that continues to the Head Abbot of the Hongwanji today is traced through her son by her first marriage.[67] Even more remarkable is the fact that this lineage comes by way of Shinran's youngest daughter rather than through one of his sons.[68] Being patrilineal since that time, the leadership has never been held by a woman, except temporarily when Kyojunni twice acted as Abbess Regent until her son, Shonyo (1516–1554), and later grandson, Kennyo (1543–1592), came of age.[69]

Returning to Shinran, though soteriological androgyny was evidently not the focus of his teaching, gender was neither a preoccupation nor a deciding factor in his form of salvation. In any event, "salvation registers" some decades later show that female and male members alike were assured of birth in the Pure Land and that the wives of temple priests worked alongside their husbands in a comparable capacity. The lists show that congregations consisted fairly evenly of women and men, mostly from the peasant classes. There are also portrait lineages (*ekeizu*, ca. 1326) depicting women, albeit subordinated to their husbands.[70]

The eighth abbot, Rennyo (1415–1499), considered as the "restorer" of Jōdo Shinshū, was also a product of his times. The social view of women had not changed. He noted in several of his famous letters that women were especially burdened by deep karmic evil as well as the "Five Obstacles and Three Submissions," concepts of which people of that era were still aware. Yet his intent, too, was not to discriminate, but to demonstrate that Amida Buddha's Vow was the only hope for all people, writing in one of his letters, "On Women Attaining Buddhahood,"[71] that only Amida of all the Buddhas would liberate them. This would indicate that specific scriptural references to the inferiority of women did not necessarily penetrate the core beliefs of either priests or laity, and that reliance on Amida Buddha's vow was the overriding point of focus. I would also add that in addition to his devotion to giving dharma talks, Rennyo was famed for his political and organizational astuteness. In his day, as today, many if not most of the listeners would have been women –hence the frequent attention paid to them in his letters. That they offered him support in many ways was no doubt beneficial to his cause, both personal and as a priest.

Given the social discrimination against women that continued in Japan, and the assumption that most women accepted and internalized their imputed inferiority even after references to the Five Obstacles and Three Submissions had faded, it is understandable that they would collaborate in the notion that they were capable of less than they actually were. Nevertheless, throughout Shin Buddhist history there have been occasional accounts of women, like Eshinni, who have expressed their aspiration to go "to the land of bliss," without mention of transformation.[72] Despite the continued existence of the thirty-fifth vow, this view is supported by the emphasis that the Shin teaching has always placed on universal salvation for all beings, just as they are (Jp. *sono mama*). Negative references to women may well have been a matter of institutional rhetoric versus actual practice and popular understanding of the scriptures.

Nonetheless, the institution continues to reflect an androcentric nature to this day. Could this be a result of priestly attitudes that were influenced by scriptures, which in turn were influenced by social attitudes of long ago? The tendency toward non-discrimination and equality are doctrinally but not institutionally grounded. Devices such as the thirty-fifth vow were expedient means that may have fit social conditions of previous eras, but are of questionable consequence in these times. It is possible that institutionalization caused not only elitism, but also an ossification of attitudes and doctrinal interpretation. In light of this, the following chapters will examine how both the doctrine and the institution of Jōdo Shinshū are perceived by female adherents in America today.

To return to Japan, feudalism was abolished as a political structure with the new Meiji government in 1868.[73] However, women became to-tally subjugated because they were placed outside of the hierarchical order of society by the Meiji Constitution and Civil Code, regardless of class. Perhaps due to this, and because fresh ideas were flowing into a Japan newly opened to the rest of the world, murmurings of women's emancipation began to be heard in some sophisticated circles. But for most women, especially in the countryside, changes to their status did not really manifest until later in the Meiji era when village life and longstanding social structures started to be transformed with moderniza-tion.[74] As will become clear in the next chapters, it was the traditional patriarchal perception of sex and gender that was exported to America with the farmers and fishermen and the first Shin Buddhist ministers over a century ago.

Feminist consciousness in Japan became established in the upper social strata around the Taisho era (1912–1926). It was at this time that Takeko Kujo (1887–1928), the daughter of the twenty-first abbot, Myōnyo, was making her mark as a tireless social volunteer and as a writer and exponent of both Shin Buddhism and the female intellect.[75] It was she who founded the *fujinkai* movement in Japan. Yet her immediate influence came too late to affect emigrant women, for the settlement of most of the first generation Issei had already taken place in America.

In tracing this history of Buddhism through various societies and cultures, it is the core doctrine of non-discrimination that stands out as a constant, drawing the attention and support of women and men from all walks of life. It is remarkable that despite the pervasive power of social and cultural traditions that has often created barriers, the dharma as expounded by the Buddha has continued to transcend time and convention and remains as meaningful to people today as it was 2,500 years ago.

As for women in particular, though it is evident that their participation in the religion depended on social bounds, society itself was in turn influenced by religious developments, often directly involving women. In ancient India, women could not actively pursue spiritual fulfillment until free of domestic duties, but the Buddha did allow a nuns' order to be established. In Sung China, the possibility existed for women to choose between the family and leaving home. Many incorporated the study and practice of Buddhism into their domestic lives, but of those who became nuns, many proved their capacity and contributed much to the advancement of Buddhism. In Kamakura Japan, Buddhism became a religion of the masses, and Shinshū could be practiced in the daily lives of the laity.

In all three eras of focus, laywomen were a strong force in providing support, both financial and devotional. They also guaranteed the continuation of a following by influencing their offspring. Common to the three societies too was the fact that they were each in a period of major transition that presented possibilities for greater liberation to practice religion, however limited by discrimination. From this, we have witnessed important female initiatives and accomplishments: the first bhikkhuni sangha and awakening; Ch'an enlightenment and lineage; and significant participation in the development of a mass movement that made Jōdo Shinshū one of the most widespread forms of Buddhism in Japan. We know of these events thanks to the few writings that exist by and about women.

Over the centuries, the Buddhist institution has undergone many changes in attitude toward women, ranging from the exclusionary to the enlightened. Alan Sponberg notes:

> Recognizing the institutional and psychological pressures that militated against the basic principle of inclusiveness asserted by Śākyamuni, one can only be struck at the persistence with which that ideal nonetheless was sustained, to be reexpressed in ever more comprehensive terms. Although the ideal expressed in that principle only rarely has been actualized within the tradition, it consistently has remained the guiding ideal.[76]

The remainder of this work will examine how this basic principle continues to guide women in Jōdo Shinshū in America today.

PART TWO

# Jōdo Shinshū Women
# In America

# CHAPTER TWO

# THE PROJECT:
# THEORY AND ANALYSIS

*There is ample reason to believe that there have always been a great*
*many active Buddhist laywomen and/or nuns in every culture which*
*Buddhism has penetrated. Yet very little concrete information about*
*these women has come down to us... If Buddhist women had written*
*the history of their own sisters or had recorded their own experiences,*
*we might have quite a different impression about Buddhism. Why did*
*the women leave the writing to men?*

Nancy Schuster Barnes, *Women in World Religions*

In the opening passage, Nancy Barnes contemplates the long history of women in Buddhism and the corresponding dearth of writing by and about them. She goes on to point out that throughout Buddhist history, patriarchal tradition has always forced women to remain on the fringes. She concludes that "the real opposition which has faced women within the Buddhist sangha is opposition to their taking positions of authority."[1] In the foregoing chapter, I demonstrated that this was true to the extent that women had to depend on the sanction and support of men to realize their spiritual accomplishments. Given the nature of the societies and cultures in which they lived, it is not surprising that they were marginalized despite any contributions they might have made. It is even difficult for us to know how the majority of laywomen participated organizationally, if at all, since we can only rely on what little was written of women and extrapolate from there.

The current work will provide an account of the thoughts and activities of American women with regard to their participation in Jōdo Shin Buddhism at the turn of the twenty-first century. Through surveys and interviews, they share their reflections, their frustrations, and their aspirations for the future of Jōdo Shinshū in America.

Such a review is timely since, similar to the three epochs highlighted in chapter one, the present era is one that reflects sweeping social change, particularly as it affects women. There are several factors involved in this transformation, including the influences of education, technology, globalization, and information exchange. With regard to Buddhism, we are witnessing not only its continuing journey eastward but also its adaptation to a new host society. Outside of the ethnic organizations, its popularization among mainstream Americans has taken place only within the last few decades, yet already scholars are speaking of an American form of Buddhism with characteristics representative of this culture. The Buddhist Churches of America (BCA), though classified and virtually dismissed by these scholars as representing an ethnic Buddhism with little relevance to American society, is itself undergoing an Americanization that potentially could result in considerable consequences for the future of Jōdo Shinshū, and not only in America.

Through the interrelated causes and conditions of its existence in the United States at this moment in time, Jōdo Shinshū cannot help but be affected by two sociological phenomena in particular that have occurred here over the course of the past century. Each has developed into an area of research that will inform this study. I will present their theoretical bases in this chapter, as each has a considerable impact on the direction of the BCA. One is the study of religion and spirituality as they relate to women – the idea that there should even be a woman's perspective, separate from the traditional androcentric one, on religious doctrine and institutional issues. The other is the study of ethnic acculturation to American society, specifically with regard to religion.

The two topics are interlinked, in that without acculturation it would be difficult to even try to analyze the religiosity of female members of the BCA using feminist religious theories developed with American women in mind, and even then we cannot be reductionist. Still, the majority of the members in question would identify themselves as American, and herein is to be found an underlying tension that has now surfaced. Has the institution of Jōdo Shinshū in America kept pace with the socio-cultural change of its adherents? Equally important, in what way does the bearing of the institution impinge upon the relevancy of the doctrine for American Shin Buddhist women?

According to some researchers, the assimilation of ethnic Japanese into mainstream American society is complete in all but physical appearance, and due to the high rate of outmarriage, it is foreseeable that visibility soon will no longer be a critical factor in identity, either.[2] Does this apply to the ethnic members of the temples of the BCA? Obviously, caution must be exercised to avoid generalization, given that there are so many variables, beginning with generational differences but also taking into account individual temple cultures and regional environments. Moreover, while many members may be "mainstream" in all other facets of their lives, the nature of their participation at the temple may almost seem anomalous to the rest of their being.

In order to explore the answers to this inquiry, I will first examine the question of ethnic acculturation as it relates both to the members and to the operation of the institution. Secondly, I will focus on the accomplishment of women's spirituality, both through practical and doctrinal considerations.

## I. ALL THINGS CHANGE: ETHNIC CHURCHES

Over a century ago, Japanese women began to emigrate to America either with their husbands or to join husbands – some of them as "picture brides." As there have been a number of sociological studies and narratives written about the first generation Issei, I will limit my comments to those which relate to women in the BCA. In fact, a large percentage of the immigrants hailed from Jōdo Shinshū areas of Japan and it was these Issei who made the request to the mother temple, Jōdo Shinshū Hongwanji-ha (hereafter referred to as the Hongwanji), to send missionaries to serve the growing expatriate population. While I will not chronicle the history of the Buddhist Churches of America in this work, available sources in any event offer little detailed reference to women members and their involvement in the institution. Despite the instrumental role they have played from the start in the development of the American sangha, they figure only marginally in the official histories.[3]

As mentioned in the previous chapter, the Issei brought with them traditional ideas about women and gender. Sociologist Yuji Ichioka relates a 1917 report of the "outdated attitude" of Issei men: "Despite changes in ideas and practices in Japan, the men clung to archaic notions they had learned from their fathers in the nineteenth century about the absolute subordinate role of wives."[4]

Obedient and generally submissive, immigrant wives laboured hard to make a home for their families in a foreign land. One way in which they could find comfort was to gather together with other women of the community at the temple. The first *fujinkai* (women's association) was formed at the Buddhist Church of San Francisco in 1900. Each temple established thereafter also formed its own women's group. In 1957, the first Annual Conference of the National Federation of Buddhist Women's Associations was held.[5] There is no equivalent organization to the *fujinkai* for men. According to Tetsuden Kashima,

> The purpose of the *fujinkai* was to aid the church in preparing refreshments or food, conducting bazaars, helping needy families, and other such necessary activities. In addition, the women's groups allowed Issei women to gather together and socialize in a racially homogenous surrounding.[6]

Their American-born Nisei daughters, however, found themselves immersed in two cultures and often had to choose between them. Mei Nakano concludes that their social circles were frequently determined by religious affiliation, and that the Christians and Buddhists among them had little to do with each other. She also notes that many Nisei attended Christian churches not only for English services, but because they wanted to be identified with things American–and the social and educational activities of the Christian institutions, even if Japanese American, were more in line with contemporary American life than were the activities of their Buddhist counterparts.[7] Bonacich and Modell agree that religious affiliation for the Nisei was a differentiator, more at the symbolic than the doctrinal level:

> Buddhism implied orientation to things Japanese and perhaps to Issei values.[8]

They explain that it provided a link to Japan and to the ancestors that Christianity did not.

Regardless of affiliation, however, Nakano concludes that most Nisei women, in keeping with their Japanese upbringing, were comfortable with consensus and cooperation rather than with independent decision-making. Her studies show that even if asked, most women of this generation would be reluctant to voice their opinions, especially if their views might threaten the status quo.[9] This behaviour may have more to do with the Japanese group mentality and reticence than with conserving tradition. However, she adds, the attitudes of many began to change after the war when they gradually had an opportunity to become politically aware and active in the community. A number of factors prompted this. American society at large began to focus on such topics as nuclear disarmament and planned parenthood. Once their children were in school, thousands of Nisei women joined the workforce and many occupations opened up to them as a result of the civil-rights and incipient women's rights movements.[10] Nakano asserts that over the past few decades, Nisei women have become more self-aware and, with their more liberal-minded Sansei daughters, many have come to modify the culturally ingrained expectations they had of themselves. Indeed, Nakano's study includes many accounts of Nisei women who are models and inspirations for independence, intelligence, social activism, and creativity.[11]

Nonetheless, however much they may have changed inwardly, it appears that the majority of Nisei women of the BCA have been reluctant to openly assert their opinions and feelings in the temple. Largely under the influence of Japanese culture until the Sansei generation came of age in the last two or three decades, traditional assumptions ruled. The passive role of women in the temple has received quiet co-operation, though perhaps not unanimous agreement, from most of the women. Perceptions of the women also vary. Some say that they conserve the appearance of traditional roles in order to encourage the men to participate in temple activities, but that in fact they themselves have more control than is evident. Differences of opinion are illustrated in the following chapters, and it is shown that the disparity is both intra- and intergenerational.

The Sansei display a very different outlook from that of previous generations, one that clearly reflects their acculturation to life in America. In their mainstream careers, they are accomplished lawyers, judges, doctors, educators, business executives, and public policy makers. They are known to Americans as newscasters, writers, and community leaders who are not afraid to share their views. For example, in 2001, Girl Scouts National President Connie Matsui, a senior vice-president of a biotech company, spoke out in defense of gay rights in the scouting organization in keeping with a broad policy of non-discrimination. She is leading initiatives "to make the group more inclusive and relevant to today's young girls ... along with corporate partners, Matsui is also working on a national technology initiative to encourage girls to pursue studies in math and science-related fields." She has been lauded by the National Association of Asian American Professionals and the Japanese American Citizens League.[12] This generation has stepped out into the mainstream of American society and it seems there is no turning back.

Indeed, by the early Eighties, third generation Sansei and fourth generation Yonsei were notably absent from the membership of the *fujinkai*.[13] Differences in orientation were beginning to surface, but in the spirit of harmony, respect, and giving with which they were raised, again women have been cautious about "rocking the boat," as one interviewee notes. However, where Nisei women have been more apt to persevere, Sansei and younger women, with various options for both spiritual and social life at hand, have quietly chosen to withdraw their involvement when they have felt ill at ease. At the 2003 Federation of Buddhist Women's Associations conference, participants of all ages were pressed to exchange views in the face of dwindling membership. The results are summarized in this report.

What can account for the changes? Though there are various sociological theories, Mark Mullins provides one possible pattern to illustrate the relationship between religion and ethnicity in his studies on the "life-cycle" of ethnic churches. Due to the limitations of space, I will use his theory as a framework for the case at hand because of the close similarities between his research subject, the Buddhist Churches of Canada (BCC), and the BCA.[14]

Mullins notes that there are generally two approaches for assessment. One reflects Durkheim's functionalist theory of religion, which posits that "religious beliefs and rituals bind individuals together and provide the social context necessary for the transmission of traditions and values."[15] The limitation of Durkheim's model, Mullins says, is that with new generations, ethnic churches cease to be effective as agents of cultural preservation due to the assimilation of congregants into the host society. Therefore, a second view sees ethnic institutions as "adapting organizations," meaning that "the process of assimilation forces the churches to choose between accommodation and extinction."[16] This "ideal-typical" model is summarized in Figure 1 as outlined by Mullins.[17]

| Figure 1: Selected Organizational Aspects of Ethnic Church Evolution | | | | |
|---|---|---|---|---|
| **Stages** | Characteristics of membership | Enviornmental changes | Adaptation required | Consequences for organization |
| **First** | Original immigrants; monolingual | | | |
| **Second** | Original immigrants and native-born generation; bilingual | Cultural assimilation | Bilingual minister and introduction of English | Effective recruitment of acculturated generation |
| **Third** | Monolingual | Structual assimilation; membership leakage through mobility and intermarriage: disappearance of immigrant generation | Goal succession and de-eth-nicization | Transformed from ethnic to multi-ethnic organization |

It is recognized that for the first generation, the religious institution plays a major role in helping the group to maintain ethnic customs, language, and group solidarity. Warner and Wittner state that a prime motivation for immigrants to found religious organizations is to pass on their heritage to their children, though this can also alienate the children.[18] The relationship in the institution begins to break down when a tension develops between the language and culture of the first generation, and the gradual assimilation of their offspring. Since religious institutions must deal on a multi-generational level, the differences are highly accentuated. However, "religious institutions are generally recognized as conservative and notoriously slow in making adaptations to changes in the social environment."[19]

Moreover, it is not always easy to make the necessary adjustments representing the second stage. Bilingual, and then English-language ministers must be recruited and trained, and additional English language services and materials must be provided. In fact, an earlier incarnation of the BCA was looking to do this in the 1930's as the organization began to establish a program to meet the needs of the Nisei. However, with World

War II and the internment camps, the initiative was largely curtailed. In addition, observes sociologist Essie Lee, the harsh discrimination of the war years caused the Nisei to turn inwards.[20] Hence, they sought ethnic solidarity in their own institutions, including the temples. Does this indicate, then, that Mullins' pattern was stalled by unforeseen and unusual circumstances? Though the Nisei eventually were able to assimilate successfully in many respects, such as occupationally and in the exercise of common civil rights, Nakano and others note that the events of the war had a deep and lasting effect on the second generation.[21]

The third stage of ethnic church development occurs when congregants experience structural assimilation – acceptance by and entrance into the institutions of the surrounding society. After the war, this did take place to a great extent for the Nisei, and by time their children, the Sansei, were active in society, complete acculturation was possible.

An upshot of structural assimilation is increased marriage outside of the ethnic group. Studies by Darrel Montero conclude that exogamous Sansei in the United States are less likely to remain Buddhist. He notes that "about one in ten of the exogamous Sansei are Buddhist, as against over four in ten of their endogamous peers."[22] Kitano found that the rate of outmarriage in the Eighties hovered at sixty percent for those of the third generation. It was projected that the trend would grow with succeeding generations.[23] This could explain one reason for the decrease in membership of younger people in the BCA.

In addition, research demonstrates that women make up nearly two-thirds of all intermarried Japanese Americans.[24] Hiro Nishimura declares that this is "because of a strong desire to escape being subjected [sic] by husbands and they want to change roles and escape the usual stereotype."[25] However, in my opinion, this would vary from person to person, both for males and females. Men could be just as acculturated; nor is it necessarily marriage that defines or stereotypes a woman. As early as 1974, in a study comparing the two, Larry Onoda found,

> The greatest changes in personality characteristics from generation to generation were among females. The females have abandoned the traditional or stereotyped roles of quietness, shyness, passiveness, and meekness for a more outgoing and aggressive role.

Onoda added that women now see themselves as more independent, dominant, expressive, social, and assertive than prior generations of women.[26] Indeed, significant to the current study, Nakano states that most Sansei women are less conscious of ethnic identity than of gender.[27] Could this influence whether women stay with the institution or not?

Mullins concludes that "generational change is at the root of all the organizational problems which confront ethnic churches."[28] Therefore, according to the paradigm that he presents, the institution reorients itself in order to encourage acculturated members to stay. In the process, it develops new goals, other than ethnic support, thereby broadening its base of relevance. He admits, however, that the ability to adapt varies depending on such factors as the size of the minority group, the source of religious leaders, and the structure of religious authority.[29]

Where does the BCA fit in this scheme and what does it mean for female members? Again, it is necessary to recognize that temple culture varies from place to place. Most of the temples are in California, where the greatest concentration of ethnic Japanese is located. Some of these temples are more conservative and ethnic in their outlook than temples in the East where we see greater integration with mainstream American society in both their multi-ethnic memberships and activities. Some temples have a significant number of "Shin Issei" immigrants who arrived in the early Sixties, so assimilation has been slower. Other temples, especially in cosmopolitan areas, have attracted new members from outside the ethnic community to join their largely acculturated members. Mullins also notes the "ethnic rediscovery" theory which argues that social alienation and identity crises produced by our modern technological society cause some later generations to return to the ethnic subculture of the temple.[30]

Regardless of membership orientation, one significant factor affects the temple environment: the language and culture of the resident minister. The development of Nisei ministers that began in the Thirties was suspended through the war years. After the war, some Nisei studied in Japan, but not until 1958 was a ministerial training center established in Berkeley at what is now the Institute of Buddhist Studies.

Nonetheless, the number of Nisei, Sansei, and Caucasian ministers has been far fewer than the number of those born in Japan, many of whom lack sufficient facility in English to effectively serve the vast number of congregants who do not understand Japanese. Moreover, these ministers bring with them the social and cultural patterns of their homeland, an outlook which has become increasingly alien to the acculturated majority. Regardless of how long they stay in America, many of them will not or cannot adjust to American perspectives. Until very recently, newly-arrived Japanese ministers had received little, if any, training in language and socio-cultural differences. The indication was that familiarity with Japanese tradition was more important than being able to communicate with congregants. To add to the difficulty, services at American temples are rather different from those in Japan, in that they incorporate adaptations developed in the United States – a factor requiring additional familiarization.

Particularly with respect to male-female relationships, there is a disjunction between the expectations of the Japanese ministers and the orientation of many of the women, especially the Sansei and later generations. This is not surprising, given that each succeeding generation has enjoyed access to higher education and professional opportunities.[31] In addition, Sansei women were raised in an age of equal rights and equal access. Successful in their mainstream lives, they bring their skills and intelligence to the temple, but experience various levels of acceptance or frustration in having their contributions and talents acknowledged by the male-dominant authority, often consisting of the minister and older male Nisei board members.[32] This can be aggravated by the innate tendency of many of the older women, though American-born, to continue to act deferentially to men despite their own obvious strengths. The following chapters will illustrate these differences.

Another factor to consider is the BCA's close ties with the mother temple in Kyoto. Though the American organization does have some autonomy in its policy and structure, and the Bishop is elected by a committee of ministers and laypeople, it still relies on the Hongwanji for the ordination, and to a great extent, the training of ministers. Ironically, when the American sangha regrouped as the Buddhist Churches of America in 1944, it was decided that the new organization should "repudiate all ties with Japan and relations with headquarters in Kyoto should be minimized."[33] However, since many of the BCA's ministers come from Japan even now, they bring with them the hierarchical thinking that places ministers above laity, and men above women. To be fair, some Japanese ministers become *kaikyoshi* (overseas ministers) to escape tradition and culture, and many have made great efforts to accommodate to their American congregants. On the opposite side of the coin, some Sansei ministers exemplify the ethnic rediscovery theory by wanting to bring back "old style and tradition,"[34] which may arguably be useful in terms of ritual, but is of questionable worth if it encourages patriarchal values at odds with the new environment, or Japanese culture over religious education.

Undoubtedly, the goals of the Hongwanji with respect to its overseas "missions" has changed over the years. In the throes of the Meiji Restoration which sought to make Shinto the state religion by diminishing Buddhism, the Abbot Myōnyo (1850–1903) convinced the government to establish religious freedom in Japan. He had the foresight to understand that the institution could benefit from internationalization, and sent priests abroad to study religion. As a result, he instituted many democratic reforms and remodeled the education system of the Hongwanji on the basis of Western paradigms, even though his reforms faced resistance from the traditional hierarchy.[35] Myōnyo then turned his efforts to foreign propagation, which coincided with both the World Parliament of Religions conference held in Chicago in 1893, and the emigration of many Shinshū adherents to America and other countries.[36] Tuck maintains, ironically, that "some of the American notions, practices and symbolisms were introduced into the Honganji [*sic*] headquarters' schemes" when missionaries returned with them.[37]

In observing the Hongwanji's overseas activity since Myōnyo's time, it appears to be more reactive than proactive in terms of propagation and direction. This, however, can be viewed as positive and liberating. Besides ministers being deployed to serve the ethnic Japanese community, the Hongwanji also supports the efforts of non-ethnic individuals in places such as Europe, Alaska, and Australia, without actively instigating outreach itself. For the BCA sangha, and especially for women, this presents a timely opportunity for them to take Shin Buddhism in America out of its routine mode and to revitalize it in ways that speak to all people.

However, Aquino accurately observes, "more and more third generation Japanese-Americans are considering leaving – or have left – the BCA… in search of more fertile spiritual fields."[38] Whether their reason for leaving is to seek religious alternatives or not, Kenneth Tanaka estimates, "Even if we took the most optimistic figure … two-thirds of the sanseis who attended the temples in their youth are no longer regular members or attendees."[39] So the question arises: Can the institution rekindle and readapt itself quickly enough?

To return to Mullins' paradigm, it can be concluded that the BCA community does not fit neatly into it. The cultural attitudes and behaviour of individual members and ministers are not monolithic. Certainly not everyone shares the same goals for the organization. A minor influx of new immigrants keeps some temples in the first stage mode, while other temples are well on their way to becoming more "American" and less "Japanese," though most temple memberships are still markedly ethnic in appearance. The number of fully bilingual and English-speaking ministers is also inadequate to cover all BCA temples.

Moreover, the organization as a whole has failed to effectively recruit the acculturated generation and instead has continued to lose members. As will be seen by their survey responses, the fourth generation Yonsei are solidly acculturated. Yet there is also evidence that some Sansei return to the temple for cultural, rather than religious reasons.[40] And while it appears that in some ways women have assimilated faster than men, they still express different views about their role in the temple, as shown in their responses to the survey. How will this impact the future of Jōdo Shinshū in America? Mullins poses the critical question for those shaping institutional policy: "Are the *religious* goals, activities, and values of this organization worth perpetuating even if it requires the loss or abandonment of its original goal and identity?" (emphasis mine)[41]

## II. NO SELF: SOME THEORIES ABOUT WOMEN

The women I interviewed, and many of those surveyed, are adamant that religion must be the main goal of the organization. Moreover, they are concerned about its perpetuation in America not only for themselves, but for everyone. Many are no longer content to sit quietly by to witness attrition by status quo. They have the ability and the will to join with the men in managing the organization back to health, and they see no reason not to be welcomed. In their daily lives, they are successful profession-als and accomplished homemakers with decision-making responsibility, independence, and authority in their own right. While some are willing to share their skills in leadership, others simply express the wish to be able to hear the dharma in a way that truly relates to their lives and their experiences here and now. For perhaps the first time in the history of the BCA sangha, the social expectation is present for equality between the sexes.

As there are so many kinds of feminism and so many definitions of it, for the purposes of this study I will borrow from an earlier writing of Rita Gross who explains that "being a feminist simply means that one recognizes and acts on the fact that women are completely within the human realm rather than in some special category unto themselves." She further clarifies:

> ... sex roles are inculcated, thereby arbitrarily limiting both women's and men's access to the full range of human possibilities ... the activities assigned to men are evaluated as more valuable, worthwhile, dignified, and important than those assigned to women, and common opinion generally agrees that it is more worthy to be male than to be female.
>
> Thus feminism's double agenda is to open all human possibilities to all humans and to lift the stigma that has been attached to women, women's work, and femaleness in so many cultures. In short, feminism has to do with promoting the essential human dignity of women.[42]

Jiyu Kennett, a prominent American Buddhist teacher, says simply, "Nobody wants to be treated special, but they do want to be treated like everybody else." The traditional activities of women in the temple are valuable and worthwhile, but are often evaluated as being less than those of men and by extension, women are often perceived as inferior. Moreover, stereotyping by gender role limits access to participation in any capacity, regardless of a person's abilities.

In chapter one, I described societies in which women were able to make some inroads as participants in Buddhism. However, they were saddled with enormous social limitations imposed on them by various gender constructs, most of which they themselves accepted. In contrast, contemporary American society is characterized by features denoting equality, as described by Catherine Wessinger:

… girls' and women's access to primary and higher education; women's significant economic earning power and ability to be active and pursue accomplishments outside the domestic sphere; daughters being valued by their parents as much as sons; women's ownership and inheritance of property; women's freedom of self-determination as opposed to being controlled by father, husband, or other male relative; and women's ability to gain status in their own right that is not dependent on the status of fathers, husbands, or sons. As these social and economic conditions become increasingly prevalent in the United States and in other countries, we are witnessing changes in the patriarchal religions that supported male dominance and female subordination.[44]

Wessinger goes on to state that if the social expectation of equality is present, women will seek out or create religions that have three characteristics: one, the divine as either an impersonal principle or an androgynous combination of male and female elements; two, a view of human nature that does not blame women for the fallenness or limitations of the human condition; and three, a view of gender roles that does not insist that marriage and motherhood are the only roles available to women. She adds that if a patriarchal tradition lacks these elements, women will begin to introduce them as they take leadership roles.[45]

The first two characteristics could easily be applied to Buddhism. First, substituting Ultimate Reality for the divine, one recalls that all dharmas are equal, the dharma is neither male nor female, and there is no intrinsic Self. Secondly, understanding the laws of karma and interdependence, one sees things as they are, and not as a construct of the mind, to which the concept of "blame" would belong. The third characteristic should be the easiest to understand and fulfill. Yet despite what is taken for granted in mainstream American society, there are still people in the BCA, both ministers and laity, who openly reflect the belief that women should be confined to the domestic arena. However, BCA women are currently engaged in the process of changing the culture of the organization, as will be seen by their comments. Again, the transformation varies from temple to temple, but according to my research, the lay leadership they have been providing in the past decade is gaining respect, at least at the local level. Paula Nesbitt corroborates the administrative ability of women in the religious institution. Her observation of several Christian traditions reveals that "across denominations, women's organizations were efficiently run and financially solvent, often more so than those run by men."[46]

Indeed, Nesbitt and Wessinger are joined by many others in the growing field of feminist studies in religion. Arising out of the feminist movement of the Sixties, scholars have analyzed religious traditions with respect to the female, and proposed new strategies for women to better pursue their spirituality. These range from creating completely new structures (Mary Daly), to blending the best of the tradition with a feminist vision and restating religious insights in the context of women's experience today (Rosemary Ruether).[47]

In the field of Buddhism, there are those who investigate and elucidate questions of gender in Buddhist doctrine and practice from a holistic viewpoint, such as Carolyn Klein, Judith Simmer-Brown and Anne Klein of the Vajrayāna school.[48] Others interpret doctrine as it relates to social systems and identity, such as Joanna Macy, who brings us back to the principle of mutual causality and the co-arising of self and society.[49] Still others, like Karma Lekshe Tsomo, mentioned earlier, engage in both scholarly and practical pursuits to bring attention to equitable participation of women in Buddhism. Rita Gross proposes reconstructing the pattern from one of institutional authority to one of democracy – an issue that is central to American Buddhism today. She proposes to do this by focusing on what is "usable" from history and scriptures based on what is "accurate." Briefly, her definition of "usable" refers to information that is of use for a feminist agenda of empowering women. "Accurate" means that the information is not androcentric in nature.[50] She, like others, reminds us that almost everything that has been written of Buddhism has been written by men, and that it has most often been delivered to us through male experience from a male point of view.

It is only in the last century that female scholarship in the study of Buddhism has come to the fore, and only very recently that women have begun to question both the way they are perceived by the institutions, and the way this relates to the dharma and its delivery. There has been a virtual explosion of writings by and about Buddhist women in the West. Notably absent, however, is contemporary literature representing the women of American Jōdo Shinshū, the group that has been here the longest by far. Some of the reasons for this can be deduced from the ethno-cultural explanations given in the first part of this chapter. Yet acculturation was taking place well before either Buddhism or feminism became mainstream interests. Judging by the dearth of female ministers, there simply is not enough of a critical mass of women in authority, either ordained or lay, to have attracted attention.[51] Meanwhile, many other American Buddhist women who are making a difference to the religion have been featured in extensive works produced by the likes of Lenore Friedman and Marianne Dresser.[52] More crucially, there have been too few women in leadership positions in the BCA to serve as role models, not only to validate women as beings of equal value, but also to encourage and empower them. King points out, "What is important is the growing participation of women themselves – that their presence has become visible and that their impact is felt, that their voices are expressed and heard and their experiences shared with others."[53] In the BCA, this is still at an incipient stage and has not become apparent to the youngest generations.

Is Jōdo Shinshū so different from other traditions of Buddhism? In some ways, it is. Shin Buddhism has no monastic tradition, and no barriers to female ordination for its ministry, though being assigned to a temple in America is the Bishop's decision. Ministers teach the dharma and perform rituals, but have no special precepts. The number of female resident ministers in Japan is rising, though it is still a relatively small percentage of the total. Moreover, Jōdo Shinshū is a lay tradition in a deeply historical and intrinsic sense. Shinran eschewed institutional trappings, and instead called women and men who studied with him in various locations "fellow practicers" (dōbō dōgyō). As mentioned in chapter one, his great-grandson, Kakunyo, created the hierarchy that has continued to this day. According to Max Weber's theory of "routinization," institutionalized religious communities form after the founding generation disappears. Their motive is to codify beliefs and tradition in order to maintain consistency, but such procedures render the institution static, in that it loses relevance to changing socio-cultural contexts. Significantly, Weber also notes that religious founders exhibit "completely unconstrained relationships with women ... but only in very rare cases does this practice continue beyond the first stage of a religious community's formation."[54] Nesbitt concludes that routinization causes "retardation of organizational change, facilitating the maintenance of authoritative control by the constituency that dominates the tradition's leadership ... [and] women typically become marginalized from positions of religious responsibility."[55] Looking at the history of the institution both in Japan and in the United States, this appears to apply to Jōdo Shinshū.

Another way in which Shin Buddhism is unique is that it espouses no formal practice, such as meditation. Instead, it encourages mindful awareness and gratitude in everyday life through thought, word, and deed. It is often pointed out that *fujinkai* women are perfect exemplars of this practice through their humble and selfless care of the sangha, though they are also the ones who insist that they need to hear and understand the dharma more.

There are many ways in which Jōdo Shinshū differs from other traditions, but these two factors alone suggest that it should be easier, not harder, for women to participate as equals within the organization. However, one factor that does not exist in "White Buddhism"[56] militates against them: not only are the authority figures generally Asian men (as they may or may not be in other Buddhist traditions in America), but most of the women are also perceived as Japanese, regardless of how acculturated they are. Moreover, if raised as Shin Buddhists, they have accommodated the attitudes of the temple, and have therefore been accomplices in the perpetuation of these attitudes. This will become clear through the respondents' comments. Their more "liberated" sisters of other schools, on the other hand, are not immersed in Asian culture. If they have had to deal with chauvinistic teachers, they have come to deal with them on their own terms, unshackled by deferential culture or sensitivity to transgressing the norm.

Thus, while feminist theories are helpful in defining problems and offering possible solutions pertaining to American Shin Buddhist women in the BCA, it is important to keep in mind that much of the research has been based on findings relating primarily to Euro-American Judeo-Christian denominations or to non-ethnic Buddhists.[57] Nonetheless, the basic premise of equal worth and equal access set out at the beginning of this section remains applicable.

Turning briefly to women in the ministry, much can be learned from the experiences of other religious traditions in America, though again it is necessary to be mindful of doctrinal and socio-cultural differences. I refer especially to studies of differences between male and female ministers. Edward Lehman concluded that significant variances between white and racial/ethnic clergy dictated keeping his analyses of these groups separate.[58] In the case of the BCA, the ministers represent not only different social, racial, and cultural backgrounds, but also a wide range of ages. Moreover, there are hardly enough female ministers to even begin to make a reasonable comparative evaluation. However, I introduce this topic because people do have notions and preconceptions of differences, and this does have a bearing on the status of women in the BCA ministry.

In a 1987 study of gender differences between male and female theologians and clergy, Martha Long Ice ventured that there were distinctions, but wondered whether women would eventually conform to male ways of professional thinking and acting. Her gender analysis was based on the following premises:

1) there are differences in cultural norms for males and females
2) all persons represent something of a mix of the norms
3) some persons are quite untypical for their sex in their culture
4) most people lean toward gender-normative development in their culture[59]

She concluded that women clergy did not become "one of the boys" as Rosemary Ruether feared, but that they were highly androgynous with a leaning toward female orientation.[60] One of her findings was that "clergywomen hold a worldview that emphasizes holism, cooperative existence, and personal responsibility for freedom."[61]

Lehman has an opposing view. He investigated the same commonly held perceptions about ministerial styles and concluded that in fact style depends on other factors besides gender, and men or women could display either stereotypical "masculine" or "feminine" style, concomitant with conditions in their personal lives. He found that there was little evidence that variations in a minister's approach were based on sex differences and where there were differences, they were slight, observing:

> More men than women manifested a liking for social power over the congregation, a rational and structured approach to decision making, and a legalistic stance in dealing with ethical issues. More women than men sought to find ways in which their congregation could develop autonomy and power over its own collective life.[62]

Not only must differences in personality and life situation be taken into account, but also the type of temple placement, whether it is solo or team; urban or rural; large or small; and the degree of congregant acculturation. Aspects relating directly to the minister are age, experience, educational and occupational background, economic circumstances, cultural orientation, and family situation. A critical factor in his or her outlook also involves the education, occupation and personality of the spouse. In fact, Lehman found that clergy couples (both ministers) displayed the least sex-typed leadership styles, and that the husband was more equitable than other clergymen in his leadership style, and more likely to be supportive of women in church leadership.[63]

Regardless of whether or not there are differences, female clergy must still deal with perceptions of reality shaped by cultural values and social objectives. Simply allowing women to practice does not reverse years of prejudice, and there is the danger that women could be ghettoized further, for example, by being offered no choices other than working with children, women's concerns or the chaplaincy, or being employed only when there is a shortage of male clergy.[64] Thus, as one experienced American teacher from a Buddhist tradition says,

> Women need to take their place as equals, not wait for it to be given to them. If they don't, they won't get equal treatment … and now is the time to do it. Whatever we do in these formative stages is going to have a profound influence on what comes up in the future."[65]

However, it is also important to acknowledge that to simply replace androcentrism with its opposite would not be an advance. Recognizing that Buddhism is about dispelling duality in any form, the institution would benefit from viewing everything in a more integral and holistic way, and take advantage of the different strengths that everyone has to offer. While female experience is different from male experience, it is also true that woman's experience also derives from many different roles, making it difficult to define normative status.[66] This is an advantage, for there is strength in diversity.

While structural change is underway, doctrine is not immune from scrutiny. In chapter one, it was shown how society affected doctrine and vice versa. Recognizing that the scriptures are merely skillful means that point the way to Ultimate Truth, and that the Buddha is said to have used an infinite number of teachings appropriate to an infinite number of seekers, it can be deduced that one should not be attached to the literal meaning of any text, nor to interpretations that may have been meant for other cultures and other times. It is all the more vital, then, that the central message stays intact.

Again, Buddhism has an advantage over other major religions, in that it is nontheistic and therefore has no male Absolute to deconstruct. The mythic images that are used to help people understand philosophical concepts arise out of Emptiness. They are symbolic and without gendered meaning because they are themselves non-dualistic. The mythic Dharmākara who formulates the forty-eight vows to become Amida Buddha takes into account the thinking of a typical man in ancient India. From a subjective point of view, he imagines all the obstructions that hinder an ordinary being's insight into non-duality. Thus, the thirty-fifth vow becomes a means to see women as people, rather than as sexual objects in female form. In addition, vows are a way to help eliminate mental barriers that some people may have concerning their own ability to gain enlightenment.[67]

For followers who understand the concept of soteriological androgyny, raised by Sponberg in chapter one, perhaps the vow would be irrelevant. Shin Buddhist scriptures do in fact mention that in the Pure Land, beings have no colour and *no form*. Amida Buddha is sometimes referred to as *Oya-sama* (parents), representing the characteristics of both mother and father. Thus, the question is whether a social construct, such as the supposed inferiority of women, gets in the way of transmitting the core message of universality. I would argue that Shinran and those who followed him were successful in conveying a message of soteriological inclusiveness, although not one of soteriological androgyny.[68] Shinran stressed that Amida Buddha's eighteenth vow was intended to liberate all beings without discrimination, but consonant with his times, he did not repudiate the thirty-fifth vow or other allusions to the "obstructions" of women. Nonetheless, followers from Shinran's time until now have understood primarily that the teaching is applicable to all, whether or not they have been aware of the existence of the thirty-fifth vow.

Shinshū historian, James Dobbins, questions the disjunction between "idealized" (doctrinal) and "practiced" religion. In his article, "idealized" refers to the orthodox idealized view of the Pure Land, where women are transformed into men, as opposed to the fundamental ideal of equality. He speculates that "women may find a more positive acknowledgment of their religious experiences in practiced religion than in idealized religion,"[69] and observes that the scriptures are prescriptive, rather than descriptive of actual practice. Hence, that women understand the teachings as universally applicable on an everyday mundane level is more meaningful to them than "the abstracted and systematized structure typically found in idealized expositions of religion."[70] Remembering that Shinran's vision arose out of his own human experience, it is possible to say that the experiential understanding of women ratifies his religious ideal of equality, and therefore their practice is perhaps more consequential than the written word.

Thus, while the thirty-fifth vow itself may not raise obstacles for contemporary women, it becomes even more important that the delivery vehicle – the institution – conveys an outlook that matches the intent. Until the present, however, it has seemed that Paul Harrison's conclusion about some Mahāyāna scriptures applies here as well:

> Although both men and women can ride in the Great Vehicle, only men are allowed to drive it.[71]

In the following chapters, American women and youth of the BCA share their thoughts about doctrine, the role of women in the BCA, the relevancy to their lives, and the ways in which they would like to see the institution develop.

# CHAPTER THREE

# PERCEPTIONS AND PERSPECTIVES: ASKING THE WOMEN

## METHODOLOGY

In the preface to *The Church and the Second Sex,* her seminal work on equality of the sexes within the Catholic Church, Mary Daly comments, "… the chief obstacle to change is lack of awareness that a problem exists…"[1]

The status of women members of the Buddhist Churches of America (BCA) and its temples is a topic that has not received the scrutiny it has warranted in the hundred-year history of the institution. In this and the next two chapters, I will explore the views of women who are currently members of the BCA to determine their perspectives on both the Jōdo Shinshū doctrine and on the role of women in the temple. Is there a problem? How do they perceive the Shin Buddhist teaching in terms of its applicability and fairness to women? How do they feel they are perceived in the temple, and what is their role? If change is occurring, how and why is it happening?

For this qualitative study, I gathered information through surveys and personal interviews. To this end, I administered two separate anonymous surveys. One was created for women members of the BCA sangha[2] and the other for BCA youth (male and female) ranging in age from fourteen to eighteen.[3]

In surveying and interviewing the women, I chose only English-speaking subjects for two reasons. One was the practical issue involved in translating questions and responses, given the limitations of both my own language ability and the scope of this study. In relation to the latter point, and perhaps more importantly, I was interested in focusing on the perceptions and views of those who were either born in America, or have been here long enough that they have a facility with English. Since social and cultural orientation is an overarching factor throughout this work, language was chosen as an arbitrary boundary of delineation, separating Japanese from American orientation. According to the results of the survey, respondents range in age from their thirties to their eighties, and represent first to fourth generation ethnic Japanese, as well as respondents who are not ethnic Japanese. Given their usual reticence, it is all the more meaningful that so many Nisei women joined with the Sansei, as well as with other female members including non-ethnics, to share their thoughts on being members of the sangha.

With the exception of the youth survey, I did not survey or interview men because I wanted to determine what women perceive about themselves and others, what they feel the issues are, and what they propose to do about it.

The women's survey was distributed at the national conference of the Federation of Buddhist Women's Associations (hereafter referred to as the BWA or *fujinkai*), held in Los Angeles in October 2003. The Federation, comprised of the women's associations of the BCA, has some five thousand members, of whom approximately six hundred attended the conference. Participants who indicated a preference for English represented approximately fifty-five percent of attendees. Not all female members of the BCA sangha are members of the BWA. In fact, the main focus of the conference workshop was to explore reasons for and solutions to the marked decrease in new membership in the BWA, which has been the traditional "women's auxiliary" of the temple. I will explore this further in chapter four.

As most of the members of the BWA are first and second generation ethnic Japanese over the age of sixty, I did not expect the survey to cover a balanced range of ages and generations of female BCA members. In fact, third generation Sansei represent a large contingent of BCA adult members, while the youth and children are generally fourth and fifth generation ethnics.[4] However, despite my initial reservations regarding the limitations of my sampling at the conference venue, I found that the survey immediately sparked a surprising response that subsequently enabled me to gather opinions from a much wider variety of temple women all over the country. Throughout the three-day conference, several individuals of all ages expressed a keen interest in the research, and gratitude for being asked their views. During and after the conference, I was contacted by women who asked if they could copy and distribute the survey further at their own temples and among friends at other BCA temples. I subsequently received more than 185 responses.

In addition, some women networked with other women in the BCA and I began to receive lengthy communications by telephone and e-mail from people following up on the surveys who were eager to share supplementary comments. This reaction in itself suggests the institution's need to address the issues and concerns of its large female constituency.[5] Certainly, there was no reluctance to participate, regardless of age. One woman explained in a message,

> Responding in an anonymous survey is a Japanese-y way
> of speaking out... They, like me, are glad someone cares
> and is trying to do something about it.[6]

The survey for youth was initially administered to participants of the Southern District Junior Young Buddhist League Conference held in the Los Angeles area in September 2003, and subsequently to the senior Dharma School class at Berkeley Buddhist Temple. In total, I received responses from 81 young women and 80 young men. Language is not a factor for this age group since all speak English fluently, usually as their first language. Responses indicate that for the most part, there is homogeneity in attitudes regardless of sex. The single difference I noted was that of self-image, when boys and girls displayed markedly different perspectives on the prospect of entering the ministry as a potential career. This will be detailed in chapter five.

Comments from the surveys, interviews, and supplementary messages are reported in this and the following chapters. Names and temple or organizational affiliations have not been used, in order to protect the anonymity of the participants.

# I. A DOCTRINE OF EQUALITY?

The role of BCA temples in the largely Japanese American community has been the focus of much examination over the years. Having passed its centenary in 1999, the face of the institution and its temples is noticeably different from that of past generations. The question of whether the temple still functions as the social and cultural center of the ethnic community, or whether there is still even a need for any entity serving such a purpose, is the subject of an entire area of study.[7]

In the case of the temple, regardless of what other roles it may serve in the lives of its members, religion has been the common link from generation to generation and from place to place. Though the chants, *gatha* (hymns) and readings may change in popularity to be replaced by others over time, the religious doctrine is the same as that first brought to America from Meiji Japan.

Through the years, the teaching styles and the content of dharma talks have come to vary widely. Kashima notes that the first Shin Buddhist temples in America were established "primarily to give spiritual leadership or comfort to the surrounding population [of first generation Japanese immigrants]."[8] As English became prevalent among the second generation Nisei, however, the institution was beset by problems of insufficient numbers of ministers who could communicate adequately, and a lack of texts in English. Thus, dharma talks focused largely on the basics of general Buddhism, which were much easier to explain than the Shin doctrine.[9] In more recent years, there have been more ministers with English-language ability, including American-born ministers, and the texts and teaching of Shin Buddhism have become more sophisticated and available, though this continues to vary from temple to temple.

How do people understand Buddhism, and especially Jōdo Shinshū today with respect to equality of sexes? Responses demonstrated a wide range in knowledge and understanding of the teachings, but the view that equality for all beings was a central teaching, with few exceptions, was fairly consistent regardless of sex (in the case of the youth surveys), generation, or age. However, respondents frequently expressed the opinion that the teaching of equality was not reflected in practice within the temple or institution. Several people confused the doctrine with the practice, and some later underlined the importance of "practicing what you preach."

Those who referred exclusively to doctrine or history gave these reasons, among others, for believing the teaching to be one of equality:

- The Buddha stated that women could become enlightened
- Selflessness has no gender.[10]
- Buddhism is for both sexes, young and old. The doctrine remains the same for all.
- The basic truths of Buddhism were there whether man

was there or not; the gender thing is created; religion is created. Truth is not.

Those citing examples specifically from Shin Buddhism made comments such as the following:

- The Eighteenth Vow encompasses all.[11]
- Amida Buddha saves all.
- *Sono mama*: Everyone is received 'just as I am' in our religion.
- From the time of Honen and Shinran they welcomed the common folk, including women, into the sangha (especially Shinran who gave up celibacy and married.)

These responses indicate a single focus on the doctrine and its universality or, as in the last example, on the historical development of the teaching as explained in the previous chapters. Most congregants are more aware of this aspect of the Shin Buddhist teaching than any other.

Dissenting voices on the subject of equality in the doctrine noted the following:

- The doctrine defines separate policies and methods for attainment of enlightenment.
- Basically, yes [men and women are viewed equally], though I find that to be "equal" we would become men sort of disturbing. I know the times dictated women be "elevated" to men, but true equality would mean we would be accepted as equals as we are.

These comments likely refer to the thirty-fifth vow of Amida Buddha, or other Buddhist scriptures referring to the phenomenon of women transforming into men in order to attain Buddhahood, as discussed earlier. Most congregants do not have as deep a knowledge of the scriptures as this, but those who are aware of it inevitably ask questions. In the case of the two respondents above, it appears that they have not received satisfactory explanations. Most disturbing is the reaction of people in this day and age who are familiar with the vow and refer to it triumphantly as proof that "even" women can be liberated, indicating that they continue to view women as inferior.

Others suggested appropriate action to remedy disparity:

- I think [the doctrine] was written at a time when men and women were not equal. Our job now is to 'reinterpret' the actual words to fit today's society.
- The teachings were written and translated from a male perspective. Therefore, we must analyze and rethink a lot of what is written and develop new interpretations of the teachings.

They understand that the words are merely a means of pointing at Truth, and that they are meant to be used as a skillful means to help people fathom the Ultimate in a language that is meaningful to them. In a similar vein, another woman commented on gender-neutral language:

- In the figurative sense, Jodo Shinshu views women and men equally. I do think the semantics of "mankind" and "brotherhood" need to be updated to reflect the words "humankind."[12]

To date, it does not appear that such reforms have been taken seriously in American Shinshū. Given the social climate in which it is situated, it seems timely to revisit both interpretation and language in order to ensure that it is appropriate to the culture and times.

More respondents mentioned the dearth of female icons and role models in Buddhist scriptures and stories. Keeping in mind that Buddhism is non-theistic and does not posit a "dualistic Supreme Being" separate from the phenomenal world, the object of veneration itself has no sex because it does not exist as an independent entity.[13] It is nonetheless common for followers to conflate the ineffable truth-body (*dharmakāya*) or the mythical (*sambhogakāya*) Amida Buddha with the historical (*nirmānakāya*) Buddha, Śakyamuni, and perceive the Buddha as being male. Thus:

- Buddha being a man may be the deciding doctrine.

It is entirely valid, however, for people to notice the relative absence of women in Buddhist writings, the reason for which was explained in the chapter one. How are ministers addressing this issue? Respondents observe:

- Women are rarely heard of in the doctrine. There seems to be little mention of women in areas of importance in Jodo

Shinshu teaching (except Maudgalyayana's mother suffering in hell.)[14]
- You hear very little of female bodhisattvas. Why?[15]
- When examples are given of women following a strict religious path, it is expressed as some quite unusual event.

Though it is true that there are few female exemplars in the scriptures, there are also the "invisible" women – the wives, the mothers, the teachers – who have enabled both notable and ordinary men to accomplish what they have. Perhaps this relates to the theme of interdependence, suggesting that followers of both sexes would benefit from a balanced and more complete view of life if examples were drawn from all quarters. Again, role models are needed not only for affirmation and empowerment of like persons, but also to illustrate the reality of diversity. Moreover, the presence of female ministers to lead the sangha is a critical factor in changing prevailing images.

Indeed, underlining the influence of positive female role models, whether in scriptures or in real life, a number of women made comments of the following nature:

- Although there are not many women ministers – role models for women – the Buddha's mother is seen in a positive light and there are services which honor the contribution of women…
- Recently, I learned of the impact of Eshinni and Kakushinni. This has opened my view of Shinran and his character. BCA celebrated the five hundredth anniversary of Rennyo. Is it time for Eshinni?[16]

The vast majority of voices, however, equivocated on equality because of the contrast they saw between teaching and practice, sometimes confusing the two:

- The doctrine is neutral regarding sexes. However, nearly all *sensei* are men. (40)[17]
- The teachings do not differentiate between men and women in the last generation – in the olden days there was inequality. (70)
- It is becoming more true in the last ten years. (80)

- Yes, except all the Hongwanji heads are men.[18] (70)
- The doctrine appears to be gender neutral, however the reality finds very few women in upper positions and... as role models or *myokonin*."[19] (50)

Many gave reasons for the confusion of doctrine and practice, indicating the extent to which social and cultural attitudes can influence perceptions in religion, even when the doctrine itself is recognized as being egalitarian:

- It is the unwritten belief in our male dominant society [in in our religion] that gets in the way of many Buddhist interpretations of the teachings.
- Culturally, I think that a male dominant society is still an influence in the religious community as well.
- To the extent that our teachings are intermixed with Japanese cultural views, those influences have different expectations of different genders.
- Nothing that I have learned in listening to the dharma suggests that [equality can't exist]. In the politics of the BCA, however, I see that there are old world, traditional approaches from Japan that do not recognize the talent and rights of women.
- In general the social rule is different for men and women, however the teaching is addressed to people, not particularly for men or women.
- It's still very male-oriented. Just recently we have gotten female ministers.

The tendency here, as was discussed during the history of Japanese Buddhism (chapter one), is for social belief to infiltrate doctrine. In the current American social climate of equality, it would seem advantageous for the BCA to identify the inherent egalitarian nature of the Shin Buddhist doctrine as being well-suited to Americans today. Yet it appears that the advantage is being lost under the baggage of a patriarchal Japanese culture.

Responses given by youth generally reflect the same understanding of the doctrine, though in much less detail. They often echo typical Dharma School teachings, or contemporary American social values:

- Jodo Shinshu treats all mankind and animals equally.
- The Golden Chain basically says that we are all equal.[20]
- Because we always talk about living things. We never say men and women.

- I believe we can all become Buddhas (or that's what the ministers say at sermon).
- Both men and women are learning the same thing, therefore everyone is treated equally.
- It's a tenet that "all are created equally" and I think that's upheld efficiently.
- There is no evidence of discrimination. Everyone has the same opportunities.
- It never says that a man or woman can do something the opposite gender can't.
- As far as I know, there isn't any sexist stuff—no polygamy or whatever…

It is notable that ministers teach that all can become Buddhas, without alluding to the thirty-fifth vow. It would thus appear that the intent of their teaching is one of equality, at least soteriologically speaking.

However, even the youth respondents perceive the same discrepancies between teaching and practice, and sometimes confuse the two, as in the single male voice denying equality in the teaching, explaining:

- I never hear of women practicing in the chants.

This indicates the importance of demonstrating a position as much as stating it if conditions allow. By this I mean that in other social eras, when women were regarded and treated as inferior, inclusiveness could only refer to the transcendent plane of reality. Thus, as noted in chapter one, Śākyamuni Buddha had no intention of disrupting social codes, even while teaching that women had equal ability to attain enlightenment. However, in contemporary American society there is a trend toward treating all people equally at all times. In fact, with equal rights initiatives and public awareness, it has become an expected norm to do so, and this is the atmosphere in which BCA youth have been raised. Thus, it could be viewed as a teaching opportunity for the Shin Buddhist establishment to *be* a tradition of equality to match social expectations.

Other young people commented:

- I believe [there is equality], even though I have never heard of any famous women. [male respondent(s)]
- There is very little explanation or recollection of women. [m]

- In stories I hear more about men, but in the doctrine there is no specification of gender. [female respondent(s)]
- No separation of sexes, but no women *sensei* [ministers]. [f]
- Yes [there is equality], because there are some women ministers, and they are the same as males. [m]
- Yes and no because the doctrine was written in a time of male dominance – and to them that's how it was, a given. [f]

In summary, it appears that with few exceptions adherents understand Buddhism and Jōdo Shinshū to profess a doctrine that is equally applicable to women and to men, and few seem to be vexed by the details of scriptures that discriminate between the sexes. Thus, Dobbins' remarks noted earlier seem to be valid not only in Eshinni's time but today as well. There is a difference between the orthodox ideal and what is understood and practiced by adherents, and it is their practice that takes precedence.

However, certain issues remain unresolved. One is the paucity of female figures as role models. With respect to Buddhist scriptures in general, this was addressed in chapter one. In the history of Shin Buddhism, respondents are correct in pointing out the importance of Shinran's wife and daughter. The eighth Abbot, Rennyo, made frequent allusion to female followers, as mentioned earlier. There are also female *myokonin*. Other than this, so little has been written about women.

The issue of present-day female lay leaders and ministers as role models will be addressed in chapters four and five. Besides the dearth of women in leadership, what is also missing is the balance of both a female and male viewpoint that is crucial to the spiritual development of everyone, women and men alike. There are simply not enough women's stories to serve as examples, especially for female congregants. Though there is nothing that can be done about the scarcity of exemplars in the past, there are plenty of sources from everyday life on which to draw for sermons for and about women. It seems odd that while dharma talks are overwhelmingly androcentric, the congregants listening to them are overwhelmingly female. In keeping with the Buddhist tenet of constant change and the importance of experiential truth, is it acceptable to ignore a large constituency simply because tradition endorses it?

The question of gender-neutral language was also raised, along with that of image – how do people "see" Amida Buddha? This especially becomes a problem in English, whereas in Japanese one can avoid the use of pronouns, though individual ministers still convey various images from which one can infer that the Buddha is both a mother and father; like a mother; or, most commonly, male. In English, the masculine pronoun is always used.

Another major issue is the discrepancy many see between a teaching that treats all beings equally, and a temple environment which does not. Respondents recognize the influence of traditional Japanese socio-cultural structures, but are no longer as accepting of them as they once may have been. This appears to be even truer for young people because of their mainstream American social orientation. It is too early to analyze the percentage of fourth generation Yonsei who will remain active in the temple or who will return once they leave. Will the downward trend begun by the Sansei continue? I only wish to note here that as far as doctrine is concerned, its credibility appears to be in jeopardy as followers observe the apparent discrepancy between teaching and practice. That members are commenting on it in such large numbers suggests the need to address the disjunction and attempt some reconciliation, since there appears to be no issue with the core doctrine itself.

As related previously, doctrine can have an effect on the outlook of an institution. In the case of the Hongwanji, as related in chapter one, the view that women were inferior took place from the outset. Mutually affecting each other, the religious institution and society continued to treat women in such a light. These days, not many American women seem to take the thirty-fifth vow literally, but the attitude of male-dominance in the temple is tangible. What effect does this have on female members? How do they perceive their role in the temple, and how do they feel they are viewed?

## II. FROM TRADITION TO TRANSITION IN THE TEMPLE: CHANGING ATTITUDES, CHANGING ROLES

Most BCA members today are Nisei, Sansei, and younger generations. In some areas, there are fair-sized populations of Japanese who immigrated after the war, called Shin Issei, who do not form a majority of the BCA sangha as a whole but may represent a major constituency at certain temples. For the most part, however, while the face of the temple is still visibly Japanese in demeanor, from young to old the outlook of the membership has a decidedly American flavour to it. Of course, degrees of acculturation vary, and not only by generation and age. Other factors depend on such aspects as whether a temple is located in an area with a high population of ethnic Japanese or not; whether it is in a rural or urban setting; and how "western" the attitudes of the elders are. Thus, there was a wide variation of responses to the question, posed to women and youth, *"Do you feel that women and men are perceived to be equal in the temple and in temple activities and duties?"* Despite the variation, however, there were far more reasons given for negative responses. The positive responses could be grouped roughly into three categories.

First, some people still felt comfortable with the traditional paradigm of distinct duties and roles for men and for women, which were termed, "separate but equal." Most of the people in this group were in their seventies and eighties. In all of the other responses to this question, age did not appear to have a particular bearing.

A second group of people expressed their perception of equality in relative terms such as, "Getting better but a long way to go."

The third kind of positive outlook was contributed by those who noted that women, mostly Sansei, now fill leadership positions in temples, at the district level, and on the BCA National Board. This is a relatively new phenomenon that began in the last decade and is gradually gaining acceptance as it becomes more common throughout the institutional system, though it is still not apparent at some temples. The development will be discussed further in the next chapter, which details interviews with some of the women in leadership.

Of the respondents who indicated a negative perception regarding equality, almost all gave reasons (whereas more than half of the "yes" respondents did not). These, too, can be divided roughly into three groups.

The focus of the first was on duties and activities in the temple. Unlike their sisters who viewed tasks as being different but equal, these women were not happy with the expectation that women should automatically do the cooking and cleaning and men the gardening and repairs, pointing out that people should do whatever they are good at without having assumptions imposed on them. Many of these women were disgruntled by the fact that they were generally relegated to kitchen duty during services, and that they were not viewed as being capable of decision-making roles in temple affairs. At some temples today women are still expected to serve tea to men who have a monopoly on temple business, regardless of the fact that many of the women have a high level of education, and professional careers in every field, including business, finance, government, education, and law to name a few.[21] For those who might otherwise choose to help with kitchen duties, a common complaint voiced at the conference was that many older women tended to be somewhat imperious, thus discouraging the younger women from wanting to participate.

The second reason for dissatisfaction among women was that they perceived the system to be male-dominant and entrenched in an "old boys' club" that was difficult to breach. It was said that the older women often acted in complicity with this arrangement, either because they agreed with it, or because they were resigned to it.

Related to this was a third category of reason given to explain inequality in the temple. Despite the fact that most members have assimilated to mainstream American life, Japanese socio-cultural values are still considered to exert a strong influence in the temple, whether by "older Niseis" as many asserted, or by ministers from Japan. One of the ways it manifests itself is in a patriarchal attitude toward women.

Following are some examples to illustrate the six categories noted above.

### I. *"Women are Equal in the Temple"*

#### i. Status Quo Traditional Viewpoint:

- Women cook and clean; men clean and do yard work and heavy lifting. Separate but equal.
- Women know that if women become overactive the men will stop participating.

These women are happy with duties and activities as they have always been and do not see the need for change. They also seem to be concerned about not making waves so that the men would continue to participate. At the upper age levels, there are noticeably more women at the temple than men. This is due in part to the higher longevity rate of women, but it is also due to the fact that women show more interest in temple activities, in everything from study classes to the *fujinkai*.

#### ii. Becoming More Equal:

- Perhaps before, men were considered the leaders. However, in the last ten years, both women and men have taken leadership roles as church President, on committees, and at the BCA level.
- The older Nisei, no, but the middle-aged are pretty equal.
- Women are welcome to participate in any area, but it is still a male-dominated institution.
- [Our church] is still a male chauvinist domain. However, it is slowly changing to include women in certain leadership roles.
- Our temple is small so we all pitch in to do what needs to be done to survive. But it appears to be a more predominantly male board of directors.
- Our temple is reorganizing beautifully. All sexes and ages help.
- Recently, a woman was added as *Komon*.[22] I think as future generations begin to lead, we'll see more equality.
- At our temple many women take leadership roles. However, I don't think this is so at other temples. I don't think this is the attitude at the Bishop's level and at our mother church in Japan.

- Yes, in most of the local activities, but not in the ministry.

Change is occurring, but at varying rates depending on temple and necessity. The necessity is sometimes dictated by the fact that younger members are leaving the temple for various reasons. For example, the BCA has a number of rural temples that have lost members to employment opportunities elsewhere. At some locations, the Nisei have handed over the reins to the next generation, which is more likely to act in an egalitarian manner in keeping with their mainstream lives outside the temple. Yet it is still recognized that while local temples are in a period of social transition that reflects the American setting more and more, the head office in San Francisco has traditionally maintained closer ties with Japan, whether by necessity or due to the personal predilection of the Bishop. Since minister placements are determined by that person, it will have a bearing on women in the ministry as was evident in the notable change that recently took place in 2005.

### iii. Paradigm Shift – Equal Ability, Equal Opportunity:

- Women have held the position of President several times and assist in all aspects of the temple and decision-making.
- We have two strong female advocates [from our temple]. They are our spokespersons.
- Women are now fully accepted as board members and chairpersons.
- In board meetings, women are listened to with as much respect as men. Men don't feel less about serving refreshments to women during a gathering.
- Our male members all help with kitchen, cleaning, and cooking duties also.

Again, the role of women in leadership varies by temple. However, a critical mass has been building over the past decade so that women are becoming more visible at every level of the organization. Many attribute this to the trend of women in society in general as well as changing self-perceptions, noting that the attitude of the BCA itself has been very slow to change. In some instances, it is reported that the women are grudgingly accepted, but having had a chance to prove themselves, they are gradually garnering respect and more ready acceptance for women in other temples. Democratization, which is a growing trend in the schools of American Buddhism, also plays a role in this acceptance.

## II. *"Women are not equal in the temple"*

### i. Back in the Kitchen:

- Men make decisions, women do cooking and hospitality activities.
- Some activities need either sex to participate, such as heavy work, cooking, etc.
- Women prepare *otoki* [special meals] and do *omigaki* [polishing altar ornaments].
- Men should help with the cooking and cleaning the kitchen more. Men and women should work together.

This is still the reality at most temples, even where women now hold decision-making positions. One of the main reasons that the *fujinkai* cannot attract younger members is that the latter no longer wish to be confined to the kitchen. This issue is detailed in the next chapter.

### ii Male Dominance and the Old Boys' Club:

While change is occurring, apparently it is not occurring quickly enough at some temples or in some roles, like that of the ministry. Part of the difficulty is having to break into the old boys' club that manifests in many organizations. This also results in the marginalization of women to powerless positions on the board. Echoing a familiar refrain from the outside world, some of the women observe that they have to fight harder to be heard and work harder to prove themselves. Equally strong is the enabling tendency of numerous women to defer to men. Many women of all ages spoke out on this topic:

- I believe most men in my age group (fifties) perceive us to be equals however, the "elders" who hold prestigious positions consider women to be helpful only, or more in the background as supporters.
- Although we have capable women, we've never had a female president – male leaders do not select females to leadership positions.

- Temple Board *komon* are all male. There are many qualified women but we are the Betsuin so it is male-dominated.[23]
- The board members and committee heads are mostly male who make all of the decisions and <u>seldom</u> show up for service. This causes me to question their commitment to the religion.
- Usually the board president and cabinet are men. Women are recording and corresponding secretaries or the religious chairperson. Most women are fine with this setup at our temple.
- Perhaps not all temples are like this, but at ours I see the women deferring to the men all the time. Not easy to take for a forty-something Sansei.
- Women have to be more adamant and give reasons why for their positions and suggestions; many times we have to be more insistent. A man just has to say something and it's taken into consideration; a woman is questioned.
- There is a very old school domination of men in authority positions.
- Equal in our temple but not in the BCA (eg. dearth of female ministers has to do with current leadership).

However, a significant number of respondents viewed their relationship with men in the temple from an entirely different angle. Their comments indicated that some women already exercised behind-the-scenes control and that male dominance was more perception than reality. Such indirect power is not unusual in the subtle interplay of relations between men and women in Japanese culture.[24] In this case, it appears that the women maintain the appearance of traditional roles to entice the men to participate.

- It is a very male-dominant society, but it is up to the women to get the men to participate. Men are the administrators (chief) but the women are the power of the temple.
- Women are more active in all facets of supporting the temple. More men sit as figureheads on the board.
- Women are the backbone and are the ones who get men to participate, but the perception continues to be male-dominated. Many of the women lack confidence to work on an equal footing with men. They seem to prefer support

positions vs. leadership ones. "Men rule the roost, but the women rule the rooster."
- Not equal, but without women, there wouldn't be many activities and duties.
- Not equal on the board, but equal in fundraising.

There is no equivocation about the importance of women in the sangha. Whether their power is directly evident or not, it is clear that they play a key role in the functioning of the temple. However, it appears that the relationship between men and women is ambivalent. Some of the women are active in inconspicuous yet effective ways, while still tolerating the traditional façade of male dominance. On the other hand, a number of women have taken notice of the inequality and do not appear to be entirely satisfied. It was possible to maintain the balance when everyone was playing by the same cultural code, but now that the acculturated third generation members' presence is being felt, the rift between Japanese and American social dynamics is widening. Apparently, some women are no longer content stay behind the scenes.

### iii. Influence of Japanese Socio-cultural Values:

- Traditional Japanese cultural norms for gender-specific roles prevail…
- Japanese culture has a lot to do with it. Men are perceived to be the leaders, but the times are changing. Regarding duties, men are relying more on the women of the temple. Actually, cooperation is the key word.
- No [women are not treated equally]; I feel this way mainly from the attitude of the minister we currently have. He's originally from Japan and he has that male-dominant personality and I really don't feel that he listens to women very carefully.

The BCA is in a period of transition in many ways. The profile of its membership will continue to become more American, even as the profile of the clergy remains essentially Japanese in character. This is rapidly becoming an issue with female members. I received the following statements from two different people who wrote to me at length to share their views:

- I believe the ministers from Japan who carry Japanese notions about women need to learn the JA [Japanese American] culture quickly. They need to understand that the JA women carry some of the same responsibilities as men.[25]
- Our previous minister was not only a male chauvinist, but favored certain people. I chose not to be involved heavily and did not really return until we had a new minister… who is very open and respects women. The ministers have to change and as long as they are trained in Japan, they will think and act like a Japanese rather than an American Japanese.[26]

## THE NEXT GENERATION

Not many of the young people had views on the question of equality in the temple. This might reflect the nature of their own participation in temple activities which could be either co-ed, as in Dharma School and the Young Buddhist League; or segregated, as in sports and scouting. Their orientation appears to be more influenced by their contemporary American upbringing in which the question of equality has normalized to the point that it is almost a non-issue in their responses to the survey.[27] Here are some of the perceptions expressed about women and their role in the temple:

- We do not look at men as being more superior than women. Everyone does their share. [male respondent(s)]
- Our chapter works equally. Why can't all parts? [female respondent(s)]
- Men and women in our temple treat each other as equals. [f]
- Yes, both do the same activities. [m]
- No, women do all the cooking and men are expected to do handiwork. [m]
- No, because I've never seen a woman minister. [f]
- I'm almost never here, but it seems that women <u>want</u> to cook and stuff; but then, it's not like manual labor is encouraged among women either. [f]

These young people are reporting their observations. Like their contemporaries raised in this society, they know they have free choice to do as they wish and indicated this in their responses. Normally when they graduate from high school, most of them will have no temple club or Dharma School class to attend. The usual pattern has been for young people to drift away from the temple at this age, and the impressions with which they leave will be a factor in their future decisions regarding religion. Unlike their counterparts in Japan, they do not necessarily feel obliged to follow the faith of their fathers. Many of the Nisei and Sansei generation before them have already chosen other traditions, or simply dropped out, for various reasons. Unresolved gender issues, thus, could become a key factor in the future spiritual development and religious affiliation of the young. Significantly, survey data indicates that many of the teens attend the temple mainly for reasons other than religion. This would be in keeping with Kenneth Tanaka's research on the "ethnic revival" theory, which shows that some Sansei parents send their children to the temple "to instill either Japanese culture or to foster association with other Japanese Americans."[28]

On the other hand, as will be seen through the interviews, a number of women involved in the current research indicate that religion should be the primary objective of the organization, and the reason for which sangha members will stay, or even return.

# CHAPTER FOUR

# WOMEN IN ACTION

While the individuals who voiced their opinions through surveys, interviews, telephone calls and internet messages had a lot to say about the current status of women in the BCA system, they were equally if not more concerned about the future of Jōdo Shinshū in America. They wanted to know that the temples and the dharma would be there not only for themselves but for future generations as well. Jōdo Shinshū as delivered by the BCA is going through an important period of transition. Attitudes about women are indicative of overall cultural and generational differences in perspective that will impede or enhance the growth or even the survival of Shin Buddhism in this country. Notwithstanding the obstacles, women are doing their part to contribute to the continued existence of the institution, and not only through the cooking, cleaning, and crafts for which they are traditionally known. Currently, some eighteen women are presidents and some twenty-seven fill positions as vice-presidents on roughly sixty temple boards across the nation.[1] In addition, female participation on the BCA National Board and its many administrative committees is gradually increasing. These developments started to take root around the beginning of the Nineties and the involvement of women in leadership positions has been growing steadily ever since.

In this chapter, I will explore the "updated" views and activities of women in the BCA. What motivates them and what will help them to achieve their vision? The growing critical mass of women leaders is representative of many of the sangha women of today and of the near future. Admittedly, there are women who indicate they are comfortable with the traditional status quo and whose contribution to the continuance of the temple is recognized by all as having been inestimable. Yet they, too, understand that the outlook of women has changed with the times. At a recent national conference of the Federation of Buddhist Women's Associations, members spent a day exploring ways to remedy a growing decline in new memberships in the *fujinkai*. I will report on some of the findings of their workshops in this chapter to demonstrate how, even in this mainstay of tradition, women are keen on redefining their focus.

In addition to the surveys, I interviewed twelve women in order to get more detailed comments pertaining to their thoughts and experiences as female followers of Jōdo Shinshū in America. Ranging in age from the thirties to the seventies, they are members of various temples and participate in diverse activities related to the temple or to the BCA at the local, district, and national levels. Some hold or have held leadership and decision-making positions in various capacities as temple, association or BCA council members; some have undertaken full time studies in Shin Buddhism. Not all are ethnic Japanese, nor were all raised as Jōdo Shin Buddhists. Others have spent a lifetime involvement with the temple. Subjects were selected based on their breadth of experience with the institution, or their commitment to the teaching of Jōdo Shinshū, or both.

## RELIGION IS THE PRIORITY

Whether the women interviewed had undertaken formal studies of Jōdo Shinshū, or acquired their religious knowledge from home and attendance at the temple, all were unanimous in stressing that the main focus of the BCA should be religion. Given the preeminence of the social and cultural activities at the temples, this is not a peculiar comment to make about a religious organization, especially an ethnic one, as described in chapter two. In fact, at some temples, members of certain clubs and associations are not members of the temple and do not regularly attend religious services and events. The women I interviewed who had grown up with the temple also regarded it as a social and cultural community. But first and foremost, they regarded it as a religious center.

Do the views of the lay leaders differ from those of the members? It is impossible to generalize in either case. Since I did not interview all lay leaders, I can only report on the most prominent concern voiced by those

I did interview. There may be other leaders who do not consider religion to be of primary importance to the organization. Likewise, as noted in chapter two, some members return to the temple to reinforce their ethnic roots, but do not emphasize the religious aspect of their participation. This appears to create some tension between members, as will be seen in the following comments.

A number of women surveyed concurred with the view of the lay leaders, that religion should be the main focus of the BCA. It is all the more remarkable that they made their comments in response to the survey question, *"Describe ways, if any, that women can serve and be served better by the BCA."*

A Sansei in her sixties replies:

- BCA could serve women (and men) better with more religious outreach. I don't attend the temple because it tries to be a cultural center as well as a religious institution. I come to hear and learn the dharma.

An e-mail message from a Dharma School superintendent trying to serve the community notes:

- My frustrations do not have to do with gender. My challenge is more on the creative side of – How can I increase the involvement level of my Dharma School parents?

And a member who is not an ethnic Japanese ventures:

- All BCA members can be better served by being encouraged to attend services. BCA would do well to engage in more outreach and public service. Raise the profile in the community so we can be found.

For these women, the mission is clear and they are counting on the existing structure as a vehicle for delivery. However, one disenchanted Sansei who has been active in the sangha and in the formal study of Jōdo Shinshū laments:

- If the BCA had a vision, it should include identifying and encouraging people to become ministers and to become Jōdo Shinshū followers. Both men and women have tried but if they didn't "fit the mold," they were not encouraged. Women have a harder time trying to "make the cut."

> The "good ole boy" network is culturally ingrained, as
> well as a long-standing practice... I don't see a future for
> the BCA but I have hopes for the teachings being spread
> despite/without the BCA.

There are a few issues here. First, there is the question, raised in chapter
two, of the overall goal of the BCA. The foregoing responses would
indicate that some people do come to the temple for religious reasons,
while acknowledging that other people come for social, cultural, or
ethnic reasons. As one person pointed out, members do not always
attend services, but they are otherwise active in the temple. It is difficult
to draw defining lines within the community because people attend for
religious, or other, or both reasons, depending on the individual. Sangha
activities also reflect this mixture in that some social/cultural groups will
support religious activities such as major celebrations and study classes
by providing helping hands, or through fund-raising for general benefit.
Helpers may or may not share a keen interest in the religious aspect.

In addition to this basic matter, there is also an issue of "outsiders"
being welcomed to the temples; another, of who gets into the ministry.
The next chapter will address views regarding the ministry. The question
of whether Jōdo Shinshū will continue in America, and whether it will be
through the BCA is paramount. The problem of attracting new followers is
itself interlinked with more than one factor. The obvious one is the ethnic
face of the BCA. Coupled with this is the covert and open reluctance on
the part of some members to encourage mainstream Americans to avail
themselves of the Shin Buddhist teaching. Furthermore, even though
this attitude may be relaxing in many places, sharing the teaching is still
problematic because a large number of temples do not have ministers
who can adequately convey the dharma in English. In fact, this is said
to be one of the greatest obstacles to retaining members, to say nothing
of adding new ones.[2] Most third and fourth generation members do not
understand Japanese well enough, if at all, to be able to connect with
sermons and lectures given in that language.

A longstanding leader in her sixties asserts that Buddhist education
for the whole family is a major issue and needs to be expanded in a way
that will attract adults and encourage them to practice. For example, she
points out that the *fujinkai's* primary function is not to cook and clean,
as many believe. It is to hear and learn the dharma, harking back to the

maxim, "Educate a man, and you educate one person; educate a woman and you educate a family." Indeed, many of the youth I surveyed, as well as women I interviewed, observed that the religious influence in their lives was passed to them by their mothers or grandmothers. Yet the women need to have access to suitable and adequate religious education and the time to participate in it so that they can truly come to understand what it is they are supporting.

The same individual recalls the principle of equality of all beings, reflected in both the Buddhist and Shin Buddhist teachings. She feels that the core people who really hold the temple together are those who understand these teachings and attend services, whether they are men or women. She concludes that Jōdo Shinshū "won't peter out," but the temples may disappear for lack of members. In that case, she suggests, "it might go back to the old days as a *howakai,* and that might be even better."[3] She points out the viability of the relatively new *howakai* growing in Europe and Australia, where ethnicity and cultural tradition is not a factor in the dissemination of Jōdo Shinshū. And, she adds, "Perhaps the BCA as an organization has just gotten too big."

## JŌDO SHINSHŪ IS FOR EVERYONE

Another woman expands on the problem of the BCA's ethnic focus, remarking,

- If we are a Buddhist religion, we can't be hypocritical. The BCA has got to change to adapt to a new wave and not be so much of an ethnic Japanese organization.

But, she also admits,

- We are getting fewer and fewer and outmarrying.[4] The Issei needed it more for social solidarity and social comfort, but it needs to change more for the mainstream. The religion itself can work; it works in America, it's just to find ways to get people to understand that it can work whether you are Japanese or gay or whatever. If the dharma is the main strength of Buddhism, then it will survive; it's just that the way in which it's propagated may have to

> change. People in America are so individualistic. They are
> searching around. Maybe Buddhism will be propagated
> more through personal contact; I don't know that it needs
> to be social… but we find strength in our spiritual solidar-
> ity through our social gathering.

The importance of having a sangha is indeed for mutual spiritual support, but do BCA temples want to include non-ethnic Japanese in their gatherings? Several of the women interviewed agreed that efforts had to be made to share the teaching with all people, not just with ethnic Japanese, and some specifically said they hoped for an American form of Buddhism. One went so far as to say that she leaned toward a non-sectarian form of Buddhism that would incorporate aspects of other Buddhist traditions into Jōdo Shinshū, making it, she believes, more amenable to Americans. If this is transgressive, she is not the first to have thought of it. Bishop Koshin Ogui, in office since April 2004, had been offering Zen meditation as well as Shin Buddhist traditions at Midwest Buddhist Temple in Chicago for a number of years before being elected to his current post as head of the BCA.

Indicative of the insularity of much of the BCA, some members are so immersed in the ethnic trappings of their religion that they are ignorant of the existence or activities of other Buddhists, even when they are located in the same districts. However, the lack of awareness occurs in both directions. One interviewee who is active at the national level marveled when she learned how much outreach other Buddhist organizations do in the community and bemoaned the thought that,

> • Jōdo Shinshū could do a lot of good in the kinds of con-
> flicts we have today, even globally, but people don't even
> know we exist.

For these women, the strength of the BCA lies in the doctrine of Jōdo Shinshū, and that doctrine is for everyone. This is reminiscent of what Shinran advocated about the universality of the teaching, a lesson that in some quarters has apparently been forgotten. A lifetime member remarked that Shin Buddhism would be attractive to mainstream American women if it were taught differently than is currently being done, indicating a general deficiency in teaching methodology affecting all. As mentioned earlier, neither the perspective of the message nor that of the listeners can be cast as monolithic, particularly in the current setting of diversity. I will explore members' views on this further in the next chapter.

One individual interviewed had been involved with the temple since childhood and then took a hiatus from it after high school. She returned not only for religion, but to "be around Japanese people." Nonetheless, it was gratifying to come in contact with converts to Shinshū because, she remarks,

- Apparently there is something in the message that appeals to those [who were not born into Jōdo Shinshū.] I begin to realize that the future and the hope for Jōdo Shinshū might have to lie outside the ethnic Japanese community. The need to translate into new languages is great because each time you do that, you have to revisit the doctrine and you have to understand the core... As long as people are interested in the doctrine, there will be some institution whether it's BCA or not, even if it's not here. I would be sad to see the demise of my temple, but the important thing is the doctrine because I think the teachings are worthwhile.

This is echoed by another Sansei with a similar background who is active at her temple. She adds,

- I think we have something that's of value that would be helpful to mainstream Americans because as Americans, we have lots of problems and a lot of it has to do with people being selfish and egotistical... there's something to be learned from Jōdo Shinshū, a different way of looking at things, seeing how we're interconnected and influence each other, so there's a value... but ministers should learn presentation skills, not just doctrine.

Moreover, she declares,

- The BCA is a huge dinosaur. We're so stuck in the past, in politics. There's no creative vision, no creative mission... I don't see that BCA is involved that much in promoting the dharma, and I think the dharma should be primary, the center of everything. There's a lot of potential for the future of Jōdo Shinshū, but we have to rise to the occasion. Somehow we need to publicize it without going out to sell it. The best thing that can be done is if each person developed it within themselves and served as examples. Collectively, we need to be more open and friendly to others and find a niche where we could be of help.

Perhaps that niche is the family orientation of the temples that many members find so attractive. Unlike Jōdo Shinshū temples in Japan or many other traditions of Buddhism in America, and more in keeping with the pattern set by Christian churches, BCA temples have an abundance of family-oriented groups, clubs, and activities, as well as dharma classes for everyone from pre-schoolers to high school students. This is partially due to the temple having traditionally served as a social and cultural center, but also because of structural acculturation to western ways.

One of the interviewees, who is a leader at both the temple and district levels and speaks from observations of her own family experience, cites the case of members who join because they have married Shin Buddhists, remarking,

- If you are not interested in your own religion, then it's easy to become a Shin Buddhist with your family because a lot of the teachings, activities, and the environment are for the whole family so you can fit in comfortably and the philosophy isn't offensive. It doesn't make you have to promise to do all sorts of things; it doesn't make you feel guilty. It's very welcoming.

She goes on to wonder whether single people from outside the tradition would really be attracted to Shinshū if they were seeking an alternative form of religion. She thinks that while Buddhism itself is attractive, an individual with more time might find more satisfaction in Zen or some other meditative practice. She explains,

- In Jōdo Shinshū the practice is in everyday life; others spend more time on the academic aspects and in [meditative] practice. We do it in a very simplistic way: you live your life and try to follow the Jōdo Shinshū philosophy [of mindful awareness]. You're not at that level where you're trying to reach perfection, nirvana, at a sustained level. You might reach the "Aha!" stage once in a while as you live your life, but it's not like you're always at that stage and we feel we're not that way because we're humans.

On the other hand, another woman offers reasons why Shinshū should be attractive, claiming,

- We take responsibility for our actions. We do not ask for a leap of faith. We are in accordance with scientific laws. We are taught to see things as they are, not for what they are not. The people who have converted find this the most refreshing.

Someone else observes,

- I see a greater interest growing [among mainstream American women.] As women grow and develop themselves, branching out more to their spiritual development (a trend I have observed), I think we will see a greater need and influx of this population into our temples. Look at the number of women [13] who obtained their *tokudo* recently.[5]

## NON-ETHNIC FOLLOWERS

What do "newcomers" who do not arrive by marriage actually have to say about Jōdo Shinshū? I interviewed four of these women, all of whom have made a serious commitment to the tradition by taking *tokudo*, the initial ordination of a Shin Buddhist priest. All of them had had previous exposure to Buddhism before becoming involved in Shinshū. All had been raised Christian but at least three of them felt compelled by deeper spiritual needs to look beyond their initial religious grounding. Two of them had been asked to leave their respective institutions as youngsters for asking questions about doctrine. One had "explored a variety of New Age religions but always ran into difficulty as the concept of a Supreme God Creator – especially a judging male deity – made no sense" to her. She discovered Buddhism through texts but could find only temples where either English was not spoken, or there were no programs for her child. Eventually, by happenstance, her son's class outing led her to a Jōdo Shinshū temple. When she heard the teaching, she felt it rang true for her, and has deepened her involvement ever since.

Another had been studying Zen, but for the sake of her husband and son, switched to Shinshū because of its family tradition. She, too, found that she identified with its teaching. She felt that Soto Zen was very elitist, with emphasis on a daily practice for which she did not have time. It began to occur to her that she was not likely to attain enlightenment, and realized that the religion was not as relevant to her as perhaps it might be. In her opinion,

- Shinshū knows the areas of enquiry of the discomforts of modern life – the general malaise, the fear, the anxiety that goes with contemporary life. In that context it has a lot of meaning and would be the biggest selling point, especially because it's accessible to everyone, without any particular kind of practice.

Another agrees that the appeal of Shinshū is "its potential to be relevant for everyday people."

However, while the teaching may be accessible to anyone once it is found, some believe that if there are problems, they stem from race and ethnic culture rather than from gender. One person states,

- We have lost many members and countless more that I have gotten to the temple who never return because we are so focused and concerned about the Japanese Americans to the exclusion of all other Americans... If the BCA does not support change within its temples and produce English speaking kyoshi[6] and kaikyoshi,[7] Jōdo Shinshū in the United States will either die or become a tiny ethnic religious practice for the elite few. It will not have a seat at the table of the exciting movement underway, now being called American Buddhism.

At least one woman interviewed has at times sensed an undercurrent of racism and feels that members' behaviour does not always reflect what they say. As to gender issues, the same person ventures that if Jōdo Shin Buddhists were to use the strengths of women, the religion would surely grow and survive because, she says,

- Women have more to offer in terms of life and giving, from the perspective of having been oppressed in any culture to some degree.

The teaching may be accessible to the adherents once it is discovered, but one problem is acknowledged by all: that the teaching is little known in America. One convert first read a reference to it in *Cosmopolitan* magazine, in an article involving *Naikan* therapy.[8] She spent several months afterwards trying to track down anyone who knew anything about this form of Buddhism, astonished to have learned that it was one of the most popular schools of Buddhism in Japan. Though she and many of her acquaintances were relatively well-read in Buddhism, nobody could help her. Finally, she happened to take a course on Buddhist-Christian spirituality at the Graduate Theological Union, and discovered that the instructor was Shin Buddhist.

I asked her what she found attractive about the teaching. She told me that she had tried other kinds of Buddhism, but neither the long hours of sitting meditation, nor the intellectually-based quest for enlightenment were for her. Upon studying the Jōdo Shinshū teaching, she was hooked:

- The relentless self-inspection and hearing are what speak to me. To see the reality of your self-nature, of your self-ishness in each moment, and to see that you're not going to fix it, you're not going to undo it... *that* felt true to me; that felt real because of death. In the face of death, you can have a lot of ideas about religion, but when someone that you love dies, you're devastated. You're not going to make it work out, you're not going to reconcile it.

As a child, she remembers having felt selfish and guilty for wanting a loved one to return to her instead of resting happily in heaven as her church told her. But, she notes,

- Jōdo Shinshū stands up in that situation; you're a human being.

She is referring to seeing her true self and accepting that she need not feel guilty about having natural human feelings. In counterbalance, she spoke of the moments of "grace" that appear every day to everyone. This balance is what, in a survey response to the question of equality in the doctrine, a member referred to as *sono mama*, being accepted "just as I am."

She further reminisces,

- Growing up in the Fifties was all about being good and doing what was socially expected of you, but there's nothing true in that; you're stuck in what's 'good' and what's 'bad.' Jōdo Shinshū felt true, so I felt as though the Buddha had grabbed me back then [when I had doubts] and years later, hearing the teaching felt like putting on a moccasin that was made for me... I know that I'm not the only heart that the Buddha touched. There are other people out there who think it's just them, but it's not. It was an incredible joy to have it not be just me. Maybe being touched is enough. Maybe other people will never encounter the teaching in a physical form. It's a very hard sell: 'Come to Jōdo Shinshū and see how completely self-involved you are and then... receive the Buddha.' I don't think so. You have to have been pulverized by something, in my opinion. Unless people have been trashed on some level and suffered, they're not going to come. But not everyone feels this way.

In explaining why she gave up on Zen, she compares what she got out of each kind of retreat:

- I went on a Jōdo Shinshū retreat, and what I learned was a completely smooth transition [in and out of my daily life.] More came into my life than being lifted up and out of my life and crash landing back in. You were removed [on a Zen retreat] from your life, from your relationships, you were relieved of them so maybe you felt better for a time, but you didn't bring anything back that was useful in your daily life, whereas the Jōdo Shinshū retreats were very healing. We could talk to the *sensei* about the Buddha moving in each of our personal lives. You didn't rise out of your life to do the retreat; you were talking but you had to go and do the dishes, too. It was in life.

In her opinion, Shinshū would not benefit from having a celebrity advocate because it is more of a grassroots tradition, "and that's actually more real, but it doesn't fit into the American thing, so nobody knows we're there."

I asked her how she felt as an outsider when she joined a temple.

She replied that she and her husband were happy to have found a sangha with which to comfortably share their spiritual quest. Moreover, she was so determined to understand the teaching that she paid little attention to temple dynamics and issues, but she always found that the members were "wonderfully nice" and she has tried to be sensitive to the culture. Because she understood religion to be such an intimate and personal thing, she was never daunted by concerns about discrimination of any kind, but she said that others regarded her as a sort of acid test, watching to see if she would be ordained or not. She noted,

- Whereas my relationship is with the Buddha, this is a temple, it's made out of people, it could go either way. But an institution does serve a positive function. As Americans, we wouldn't even have anything we could read of Shinran's writings if it weren't for the institution. So it's not just negative, with people making trouble.

These women demonstrate that Jōdo Shinshū has universal appeal, and despite the obstacles, they can and do adhere enthusiastically to rthe religious aspect. So, while some temples continue to represent the first stage of Mullins' ethnic church paradigm, other temples are clearly moving into the third stage of adaptation due to both acculturation of ethnic members and the participation of non-ethnics from the dominant society.

## WOMEN ON THE BOARD: KEEPING JŌDO SHINSHŪ ALIVE AND RELEVANT IN AMERICAN SOCIETY

The institution, then, is vital to growth and many women advocate a return to a stronger focus on religion. But another prominent leader questions the apparent lack of institutional direction, stating,

- The sad part of it is that our generation grew up with no doctrine and our Dharma School was to listen to sermons that we didn't understand because it was in Japanese. We've got to have more dharma classes for adults. That's where we're lacking.

Politics is the bane of many an organization, but in the BCA, perhaps because of the religious grounding of much of its current executive, the board "gets so involved in organizational things and religion gets lost along the way. They treat it as two separate things because they want to survive as an organization."

It is no secret that members across the country are less than complimentary about the national body and question what benefits flow from its existence. One of the women who wrote to me even refuses to have any part of her temple membership apportioned to the BCA, stating that her frustrations are not due to gender, but to her perceptions about the BCA leadership.[9] Still, because she is an ardent believer in Shin Buddhism and its dissemination, she does what she can to promote it. She is not alone in taking action, despite the obstacles. From temple presidents to regular members to a number of representatives on the National Board, women of all ages have ideas and aspirations for the revitalization of Jōdo Shinshū in America.

First, they wish to address the gender issue in particular. Women surveyed say that they could serve and be served better if the BCA made a public policy of gender equality and demonstrated this through its actions. For example, one person suggests an ongoing dialogue to ensure equal treatment. Another recommends workshops or seminars for ministers and BCA leaders on the topic of attitudes, with the aim of bringing them to

- respect and trust that [women] genuinely care about Buddhism and the future of the BCA; to appreciate the fact that they have a background in homemaking and rearing children, as well as education and work skills.

Indeed, domestic experience is a useful attribute to have in management, not to mention the professional skills that women can bring to the table. In a recent news article pointing out the number of women in prominent positions in California business and politics, it is noted,

- Women's skills have been so underutilized. All the things we do within the family unit–organizing things, shifting and juggling priorities, putting out fires and preventing new ones–these are the skills a leader needs.[10]

It appears that this could prove useful to the BCA.

One individual finds the "male chauvinism... totally unacceptable," but she supports her local temple "since we are much more open to women's ideas, contributions and leadership." She feels that her temple is more progressive than the BCA but still lags behind the mainstream because "Japanese American women are still quite passive." The observation is made that "Issei and Nisei women are reluctant to speak up." Another person simply reflects one of the fundamental principles of the teaching, saying, "They can be better served by being accepted for who they [women] are."

Many women stress the need for an increase in the number of women in leadership as well as in the ministry. They point out the shortage of female role models in these areas. A young Dharma School superintendent claims that the traditional deference to men has been a self-imposed obstacle but declares,

- with the advent of equal rights, women's rights, NOW, and Title IX, women are expecting and assuming the equal treatment that the BCA needs to recognize.

She would like to see women leaders exercise their capacities beyond the *fujinkai* and Dharma School where they have traditionally been relegated. And despite the growing number of women heading up temple boards, a perusal of the BCA Directory indicates that other than in these positions, women almost only appear, and then overwhelmingly, as board secretaries.

A member who has been heavily involved in the temple all her life and is familiar with the national network believes that the temples with substantial female representation on boards have turned almost completely to English as the operating language. Along with this comes a leaning toward American culture. For example, at one such temple, refreshments are no longer supplied by the *fujinkai*, as is traditional in many temples, but by a *toban* system involving all family members.[11] In fact, says a temple representative,

- the *kimochi* [feeling] here is such that people who are not in the *toban* group will pitch in ... people rise to the occasion.

A woman elder comments that men are also praising the value of female board presidents and the fact that

- women's organizational skills are much better than men's and they know how to work with people socially, too.

Another person observes that women in mainstream occupations have proven that they have the analytical and strategic skills to make a difference in the workplace. It must not be forgotten that many of the women members are career women and accomplished professionals in their own right.

At a temple where a history of more than one female president is already forming, a witness to this change says that board meetings have become more efficient while actually focusing more on necessary details that were previously neglected. She recalls,

- Board meetings used to go for hours and hours… but you have to be realistic in this day and age and be more efficient to encourage people to come to the meetings.

She points out that the women are either working full time or may be retired, but all are busy with household duties, families, and other community work.

There is a difference in style between Japanese- and English-speaking members at meetings:

- The English-speaking members are freer at expressing how they feel openly at a meeting. The Japanese-speaking member might do it on a one-on-one basis, but in a group they just seem to clam up, and if it's in the negative, all the more. When it comes to voting there is a real difference. I think it's a cultural thing, whereas Nisei and Sansei don't care; it's nothing personal. They'll vote against something, or they'll vote for it even if they're the only one.

Another woman bemoans this fact:

- The women who could really share a lot are the older women who are so shy and humble. They have so much inside of them and they don't realize it.

There is another silent group that could make a difference if they knew things were changing for women. These are the women who no longer participate in BCA or temple activities.[12] I was told,

- There are Buddhist women out there who don't show up or aren't actively involved. It's not that they are against Buddhism, it's that they're against the way the organization is structured and the position of women. What happens is that because they're raised Buddhist and Japanese, a lot of them feel the way they should react is to be polite and not cause problems by speaking out and saying things that might make other people feel uncomfortable or unhappy.

The person who related this has a Sansei relative who fits this profile. She added,

- If she were with contemporaries [outside of the temple community] she would voice her opinion because the atmosphere would be give and take.

She went on to say that she knows many members who purposely keep to the periphery so as "not to cause trouble." They seized the opportunity to speak out anonymously through this research because they still have deep feelings for Buddhism and for the community.

To remedy the inequity in representation, one step the active members propose is leadership training for women, whether at the local level, nationally on the BCA Board, or through such opportunities as the national *fujinkai* conference. Although there are larger numbers of women on the national board and national council, one experienced individual relates,

- They lag behind in more meaningful leadership positions. Of the two women on the BCA Executive Committee, both have lesser roles – one is in the traditional role of secretary, the other is an auditor.

She suggests that training include the history of the BCA, personal traits that make men and women different, interpersonal skills, speaking skills, and assertiveness training.

Yet women do arrive with strengths. It is said that women do their homework before meetings, and also take initiatives. For example, one female temple president made the time, despite the demands of her job and family, to put together a handbook to guide new temple presidents. As a consequence, it is remarked,

- It would be helpful if there were more women like her who could bring more understanding to the process.

Another interviewee shares this perception:

- Women in leadership act more often than not in an attempt to address a need for change and to solve problems rather than just trying to be at the top… Men in temple/ BCA leadership roles have a greater tendency to be a result of someone wanting to be in the spotlight rather than viewing the position as an opportunity to make an improvement.

She adds,

- I think much of the future of Jōdo Shinshū and the BCA depends on women. I truly believe that if it weren't for women in the temples, there wouldn't be any temples. The men may have been the 'leaders' but the actual operations were in the hands of the women. The major functions of the temples rest in the hands of the women.

In chapter two, I discussed differences in style between male and female ministers. Lehman concluded that while people perceived that there was a difference similar to the one cited above, in fact the differences, in reality, were slight. Since there have not been many laywomen in leadership positions, it is difficult to assess whether the same holds true for the laity. Certainly, there are men who have acted primarily in the interests of the organization, just as there may be women whose aims are self-serving. It is possible that since the entrance of women into these positions is relatively recent, they are still making their mark and proving themselves, whereas many of the men may have settled into a routine of complacency. A couple of the women drawing on personal experience mention,

- The women, unless you are a BWA representative, are less reluctant than the men to speak up and push on issues, and ask questions to get answers.

There is a perception that the BWA president has always played a conservative role on the board, perhaps in keeping with the image of the traditional role of the *fujinkai*. Now women in other board positions are being more aggressive. In this way, a number of items have been investigated or resolved. One was the creation and implementation of a long overdue sexual harassment policy, in the wake of an incident involving Reverend Carol Himaka a decade ago.[13]

So far, the experience of female leaders in the BCA mirrors that of women in decision-making positions everywhere. One person notes,

- I think I am constantly running into barriers and frustrations in the temple/BCA due to being a woman. If I say something at a board meeting or speak out... I am often frowned upon by the men. They see me as a bossy, pushy woman. However, the same thing said by a man is more likely to be seen as being assertive and 'having guts.' It is more likely to be viewed as a leadership quality. Men on temple boards tend to like more passive styles and wait for things to happen rather than make them happen. They see a problem and wait for someone to fix it rather than attempt to delegate it out.

Explains a retired educator of high rank,

- It's a fine line that we women walk in leadership roles. If we're too strong, it seems to turn off some people. If we're too weak, we're seen as too weak and our voices are not listened to. We have to take the middle path and be strong, but at the same time have this give-and-take. It's a mistake to take on every issue that comes up because people stop listening. This can make you feel frustrated and you lose support.

She also observes that many other women are reluctant to speak up because they are afraid of being shot down, but she does not take the exchanges with men personally "because we're working toward the same goals." She respects the fact that some women are not interested in leadership and enjoy cooking, but she feels people should be aware that some women aspire to and are capable of more responsibility.

To help them to become more politically astute, she is mentoring younger women to maneuver into positions of responsibility. She says this is easy because their mindset differs from that of the older women. However, the problem is that they are also very busy.

- How do you reconcile a busy life, being a wife, mother and career person with trying to do all this volunteer stuff, too? It's harder for a woman. It's not so equal in sharing of the household duties.

Both she and another senior leader mentioned that their husbands were very supportive in helping with family obligations when their children were young. A temple president noted that this seemed to be the norm with the Sansei generation, due to the influence of the mainstream American society in which they were raised.

These people know the challenges faced by women breaking new ground. One of them surmises that they are more likely to follow up on issues, explaining,

- There are so few of us that we really need to prove ourselves and succeed. We'll do more, go the extra mile where a man doesn't have to do it. You always keep in the back of your mind that you don't want to fail because of the idea that failing will discourage other women. This is just as true as in the professional world.

It is also possible that leadership experience gained serving the temple or the BCA will transfer to the workplace, thereby empowering women further.

But some women also contribute without a lot of visibility. A former temple president who exemplifies this says,

- I don't mind doing anything for the church on any level, but it's got to be productive. If it's just to get your name recognized, it's not worth it. You realize that one person doesn't do it, though I did stick my neck out and do a few things because I saw the need.

Either way, it is evident that the focus is on caring for the whole group as opposed to attaining power or attention for oneself. It would be useful to research similarities and differences in goals, objectives, styles and perceptions between women and men in leadership in the BCA, to determine if generalizations based on sex can be made. I would suspect that other variables, such as personality, experience, age, education, and profession, not to mention religious dedication and cultural orientation, would also influence an individual's performance of duties.

# THE BUDDHIST WOMEN'S ASSOCIATION: AT A CROSSROADS

Regardless of style, there is an expressed urgency among the women surveyed to take action whether as an individual or as a group. One leader claims,

- The Issei would give their last five dollars to the temple, whereas young people want to see what you're going to do for them. They are educated and we have to respond. If not, we will lose them.

One thing she proposes is to co-opt the *fujinkai* into making the most of its reputed influence, asking,

- Why is it that everyone says the *fujinkai* is the backbone and has all the money, but when the rep brings up an issue at the National Board, people don't even listen. If they have that much power, why aren't people listening? It's going to take a lot of strong women to change tradition and the perception of the BWA. They themselves have to do it. The men can't do it for them. They can become more interested in the issues and articulate them at the Board and the National Council meeting.

Indeed, it is up to the women to be more assertive, and not wait for desired changes to simply happen. Rita Gross compares this to the days of Śākyamuni Buddha:

Women, not men, are usually the ones who push for non-patriarchal gender arrangements. This is not necessarily due to ill will on men's part, but simply to lack of experience and consciousness ... It's not their issue and not enough is at stake for them.[14]

She adds that while some men react in hostile and unsympathetic ways, there are also those who support women's initiatives once they become aware of them.

At the practical level, suggestions for and by the members of the *fujinkai* herald the will to change in order to be of greater benefit to all. At the 2003 national conference in Los Angeles, some six hundred members of the BWA gathered to discuss action to be taken to address their rapidly declining numbers. The women split into ten workshops that allowed input from everyone. Not surprisingly, the outcome of the four Japanese workshops was rather different from that of the six English workshops. The Japanese groups did mention that members had forgotten that their primary purpose was to hear the religious teachings. Otherwise, suggestions for action were much more vague, reflecting a position of status quo even while acknowledging the criticisms.

On the other hand, the English workshops produced an astounding range of new ideas for revitalization. There were older members who argued for keeping activities and duties intact, and this was respected. But the resounding chorus heard from many was, "not just kitchen work!" Younger people wanted to change the *fujinkai* label altogether because it signified cooking and cleaning. This image is often stated as a deterrent to many people who are otherwise active in their volunteer work at the temples. One temple president told me that she hesitated to join because the activities did not suit her interests. "The *fujinkai* means my mother," she explained.

Appellations aside, everyone agreed that the organization should make promotion of the dharma its primary goal. They called for more seminars and workshops to be given by "broadminded and outgoing" ministers who could communicate well and tell them how to incorporate the teaching into their daily lives. On this note, one former *fujinkai* leader told me that traditionally, guest panels consisted of male ministers who simply gave mini-sermons to which women listened passively. She found that conferences became much more meaningful if ministers' wives, female ministers, or laywomen were invited to speak because there was audience interaction and a closer experiential connection. The norm, though, has been for the BWA to defer to the wishes of the ministers, almost all of whom are male.

Members also called for educational seminars on a variety of topics, including health care, family issues, women's issues, professional and career issues, leadership, finances, marriage (including intermarriage), divorce and abuse. This correlated with their American lifestyles. However, there was also continuing interest in learning traditions such as cooking, crafts and cultural arts.

Reflecting American society, the women wanted interfaith events and activities that acknowledged ethnic diversity. Moreover, it was felt that the BWA should sponsor more activities geared towards couples and families. In fact, many groups proposed that the association no longer be confined to female membership, but that men be encouraged to join as well. Another proposal was to engage in more community and social outreach. It appears that there is evidence of the third stage of Mullins' paradigm happening here, as attitudes and activities merge with members' mainstream lives outside the temple.

Concerning kitchen duties, some local BWA chapters have found a solution to the shortage of time: they now use instant foods or simply order out. While tradition is lost, this is the concession to having time to attend services and participate in other temple activities. Instead of sushi and teriyaki chicken, these are sometimes replaced with sandwiches, pizza and donuts. At the more traditional temples, the core of people who usually do the cooking is getting older and smaller, with few replacements in sight. Perhaps in response to this, some women have requested that accommodations be made to permit the accompaniment of children and grandchildren, especially when doing volunteer work.

In any case, a lot of women said they wanted to be doing more than cooking and organizing their next conference as a social event. Many felt that a three-day conference was an excellent opportunity to learn the dharma and hear motivational speakers on significant issues in their lives. If this took place, according to the surveys, more women would join them. People perceived their meaningful participation as changing to a religious focus, which might or might not include the same extent of service and social aspects as in the past.

Progressive thinkers proposed that the separate organization be abolished altogether, since the sangha should be considered as one entity working together. To address women's issues, one local board member suggested that the executive board at the temple include a vice-president for women's affairs. This way, the person would have authority on behalf of women's interests, but at the same time, she would be involved with the whole temple and the entire sangha would work together in the spirit of non-differentiation. She recalled that the *fujinkai* came into existence because of the traditional role that women used to play in the temple. Indisputably, times have changed.

Whether the *fujinkai* will continue to operate as a separate group remains to be seen. Two of the younger members I met said that they did not mind current activities, but would welcome implementation of the suggestions as well. However, there are not many women under the age of sixty in this venerable organization, a fact that speaks for the absent majority of younger BCA members. Certainly, there are women who argue for the importance of having a group that caters to the interests of women. Those who advocate making the association more couple- and family-oriented concede that there may be occasions when women may wish exclusivity, but those events could be decided on an "as requested" basis just as for any other interest group, they say.

In this chapter, I have explored the expanded roles that women are playing in American Jōdo Shinshū life. With those roles have come new thoughts and ideas for making the temple and the institution of the BCA stronger and more relevant, not only for women, but for everyone. Of course not all members share the views of the women whose opinions and observations are illustrated here. However, these women are active forces in a system that many of them feel is stagnating and in danger of disappearing. What seems to drive them is a powerful belief in Jōdo Shinshū, and the will to keep it alive in America. Their grandmothers demonstrated the same dedication when the request first went out to the Hongwanji to send overseas missionaries from Japan. Over the course of a century, women have done what was socially and culturally appropriate to keep the temple going, in accordance with the times. It appears to be no different for American Shinshū women today.

# CHAPTER FIVE

# THE SHIN BUDDHIST MINISTRY IN AMERICA

One topic that many women pointedly raised in discussing the future of Jōdo Shinshū in America related to the ministry. Numerous comments were made about the suitability of BCA ministers to the current membership, involving questions of culture, language, and age. In addition, I asked for and received feedback on the issue of women in the ministry. Since the installation of a new Bishop in 2004, the number of female ministers serving in the BCA has more than doubled, from three out of approximately sixty active ministers, to seven. One of them, having served for a time as a temple minister, is at present engaged in hospital chaplaincy. Another serves as both a temple minister and holds the distinction of being the first Buddhist chaplain to serve the U.S. military.

In this chapter, I will report not only on women's perceptions of ministers and their attitudes, but also on what they see as the role of the minister in their temples today. One of the more striking outcomes of the research, though perhaps not surprising, was the insistence that ability was not predicated upon the sex of the minister. If anything, the overall opinion indicated that the inclusion of more female ministers would add much to the organization, not only in terms of numbers, but also as a means of enhancing the teaching through offering alternative perspectives and approaches. The 185 women who responded to the survey, with few exceptions, felt that women should be encouraged to pursue the ministry. The 161 youth surveyed were unanimous in support of women in the ministry. It is evident from their detailed responses that because of their social orientation, they take equal employment opportunity as a given in any profession, including the ministry.

In order to get a view from "the inside," I also interviewed women ministers of Jōdo Shinshū in America. Two of the BCA ministers agreed to be interviewed, and I asked three women serving in other organizations to add their perspectives as female ministers of Jōdo Shinshū in America. I will report on the comments of the latter as they related particularly to their position as Shin Buddhist ministers and as women in the ministry. Though most did not request anonymity, I have chosen not to use names in this study.

## THE ROLE OF THE MINISTER

In both surveys, respondents were asked what they thought the main duties of a minister were. There was a wide range of responses from the predictable to the uncommon. One eighty-seven-year-old Nisei felt that the minister should teach Japanese, as some did long ago. Summarized below are the most frequent responses, in order of recurrence.

1. To teach the Buddhist doctrine. [Many also specified the Jōdo Shinshū doctrine. This was by far the most common response in both the women's and the youth surveys.]

2. To provide religious leadership and spiritual support and guidance.

3. To officiate services and rituals, including regular services, memorials, funerals, weddings, and special religious days.

4. To give good dharma talks/sermons in easily understandable language. English should be mandatory. The talks should be relevant to members' daily lives.

5. To be devoted and friendly to the sangha and be available to everyone without preference. To provide support during times of crisis or grieving. To be a sympathetic listener.

6. To give counseling, advice, and guidance to those in need.

7. To do outreach. [It was unclear how many people referred to religious propagation and how many to community outreach in terms of social welfare.]

In addition to these functions, people also list various administrative duties, such as working with the board, participating in temple activities, and helping with temple growth (membership and financial).[1]

Finally, a minister is expected to be a role model to the community and to be sociable, pleasant, diplomatic, warm, friendly, compassionate, and understanding of all viewpoints. Moreover, he or she should teach by example, constantly striving to increase his or her own understanding of the dharma while maintaining religious practices and traditions. However, the minister should remember that "he is human like everyone else, and be a real person."

Regardless of how well a minister fulfills his or her duties, however, people look for a sincere heart. Elaborates one Sansei,

- My ideal minister is one who is truly interested in his/her congregation above self-interests. I feel the ideal minister is one whose whole heart and energies should center on the needs of the congregation and the spreading of the dharma. Even though I could not understand some of the Issei ministers, I could feel and sense their concern for my well-being. I may not have understood their sermons, but I think a lot of times I knew what they were conveying. Sometimes now when I listen to some ministers giving a dharma talk, I feel they are just going through the motions. They are saying the right words, but there really is no heart or feeling behind it – the words are not sincere. We remember not what someone says, but more so how they say it.

One individual said that members should not decide the minister's duties. Two people, a Nisei in her eighties and an Issei in her sixties, included ministers' wives as having duties such as "taking care of flowers and tending to the church."[2] By way of brief background, as recently as 1977 in his detailed sociological and historical study of the BCA, Tetsuden Kashima devoted a whole section to "the minister's wife and family," in which the wife is regarded as an extension of the minister and expected to perform what amounts to a full time job at the temple by virtue of marriage.[3] In Japan, ministers' wives (*bōmori*) are often ordained and assist in the functioning of the temple.[4] Besides cultural differences, however, it is important to note that the Jōdo Shinshū temple in Japan usually belongs to the minister; it is both his or her home and business, which is customarily inherited by the eldest son. In the BCA, the minister is considered to be an employee of the temple. Traditionally, wives have nonetheless fulfilled their role as *okusan*[5] both by choice and out of a sense of duty. Some of the wives are ordained but do not have *kaikyoshi* (overseas missionary) status, so are prohibited by the BCA from performing services in the United States. However, they lend a hand in many other ways. Some wives, especially Americans, have busy careers of their own and support their husbands' activities and the temples to the extent possible or desirable. This, too, is partially due to differences in generation and culture. A Sansei member in her forties felt that it should not be an expected role. Attitudes vary from temple to temple and member to member. However, such thinking is also related to the times in general, since churches of other religious traditions in America have undergone comparable changes with respect to roles of the clergy and their spouses.

The youth surveys produced a similar list of duties for ministers, but demonstrated an even greater belief that the minister should be a paragon of virtue, spreading the teachings of Buddhism, living right, exemplifying morality, bringing honor to the sangha… and being enlightened. Displaying a somewhat less exalted view, one young woman stated,

- I believe a minister is a figure of understanding for the congregation. I see the minister as a person who will not judge you, but instead befriend you.

Other teenagers felt ministers should be open-minded to all situations. This is particularly significant given that flexibility and change appear to be needed in this time of transition for the sangha. That the young people specified this is an indication of what is important to them.[6] As is normal in America, the minister is one of the key factors in an individual's decision about where he or she will practice religion, whereas in Japan, people tend to be more bound by family tradition.

These are the expectations of women and youth for their ministry. Some of the women interviewed supplied further details regarding the kind of minister who could best serve today's sangha, based on their experiences and observations:

- A minister who can speak fluent English.

- An expert on the dharma, who can impart it in a meaningful way.

- Propagation is important but human relations are imperative. The talks have to hit us as human beings or it doesn't mean anything at all. Be able to talk to us on a personal level, not from up there. We're not looking for answers, but direction.

- An involved teacher who recognizes his/her flaws and, by example, strives to improve…teaching and explaining by personal experience.

- Someone who is open to innovative approaches of teaching the dharma. I lean towards creating an <u>American</u> <u>Buddhism</u>, a spiritual center without sect.

- A minister who will make Jōdo Shinshū more user-friendly, without a lot of Japanese terminology.

Evidently, members are manifesting their acculturation and are looking for a minister who can communicate in a meaningful way with them without acting superior. They are also looking for ministers to adapt the teaching to America, and explain it in words that they can comprehend. This does not necessarily mean that foreign words cannot be used. Many Buddhist words in Sanskrit, such as *dharma, karma* and *nirvāna* are used (sometimes incorrectly) by Americans in everyday life. However, it is important that ministers be able to convey the meaning of Japanese terms like *shinjin* in understandable English. Such communication is essential if the teaching is truly Buddhist, for it must apply to all beings, not only to those who understand Japanese.

One of the women leaders commented,

- Every minister has strengths and weaknesses, but the strength we want to build on is the minister's ability to connect with the sangha so that they're learning. Just that alone will bring them back into the fold.

Some of the comments reflect concerns about the social and cultural awareness of ministers, especially on women's issues:

- We need a minister who is receptive and sensitive to

the cultural and social challenges of American women in transition.

- A person who is blind to gender roles and encourages people to participate in the church based on their skills and knowledge.

- Ministers have to be knowledgeable and sensitive to gender issues, such as sexual harassment and inappropriate remarks to or about women, and be able to deal with such problems as soon as they arise.

One respondent elaborated on the need for ministers to be trained in counseling, a hope shared by many of the women surveyed. At present, very few ministers have either the training or the desire to counsel members on personal matters. Since ministers in Japan are not called upon to fulfill such a function, it is not included in the seminary training there. Perhaps this is due to the fact that most of the training centers on doctrine and ritual, rather than on relating to the sangha. In any event, were counseling skills taught in Japan, the question would then arise as to how applicable such training would be in the United States, given the differences in social and cultural values. Yet members note that this service is sorely lacking, explaining,

- In the United States, this is what they do. It's a very common thing to see your teacher or doctor or minister for counseling. So if your minister cannot give you help and doesn't have a clue, it's terrible. I know of [a member] who had marital problems and went to his minister to get help. The minister couldn't do it, so he went to a Christian minister and got counseling and advice and now he goes to a Christian church. To be turned off by your own minister is not going to be helpful at all to Buddhism in America. This is another course that ministers are going to have to take, and I don't mean some ministers who are interested, I mean every minister because every temple will have people who will request counseling. It's an opportunity for every minister to teach because Buddhism can help you in these kinds of issues... but they're not going to do it if they can't even begin to talk about marriage or problems with children. And if you don't know English, you've got to master it. It's foremost.

Members expectations of the minister s role is based not only on longstanding temple convention, but is also informed by social norms in the surrounding environment. With alternatives readily accessible, people choose what satisfies their needs, and as products of a pluralistic society, are not bound by family religious tradition. Repeatedly, people emphasized that the clergy had to reflect the needs of the sangha here and now in America.

On this note, since it is the Bishop who plays a decisive role in everything from selection and placement of ministers to religious leadership to policy-setting, women also volunteered opinions on the kind of person who could best lead their American sangha:

- We have to get an American-born Bishop because of our culture.
- Someone who is really close to the laypeople and communicates with them.
- Someone who respects and listens to women as well as men.
- Someone who can articulate a vision; who makes statements and takes stands.
- A leader who urges temples to take on issues that involve our sangha.
- A religious leader who can move us forward into an American form of Buddhism.

Clearly, J do Shinsh in America has turned a corner and can no longer be considered the "baggage Buddhism" of a century ago.[7] It is still in the throes of a major transformation, but there is no turning back. If the religious tradition is to survive and flourish, the profile of the sangha, it would appear, is demanding that the delivery system change.

## WOMEN IN THE MINISTRY: PERSPECTIVES OF LAITY

If it is true that "half of the Buddhist teachers in the West are women,"[8] then one of the areas in which J do Shinsh lags behind many other traditions of Buddhism in America is in the number of female ministers. Prior to the seven women who are currently serving the BCA, historical accounts show that only five other ordained women have served the institution, beginning in 1955.[9] What can explain the dearth of women teachers in a religious tradition that prides itself on the equality of all beings, in a country that takes equal opportunity as a given?

Unlike some schools of Buddhism, notably in the monastic traditions, ordination of women in today's Nishi Hongwanji is not a major issue. From the beginning, when Shinran married and had a family, women played instrumental roles in the development and maintenance of the Jōdo Shin teaching. However, in the eight hundred year history of the tradition, the first female ordinations did not take place until 1931.[10] The latest records available (March 2002)[11] show that 9,087 women in Japan, representing 29.2 per cent of the total, now hold the initiatory *tokudo* ordination rank. The full ordination rank of *kyoshi* was held by 18,640 people in Japan during the same period, of whom some 11.3 per cent, or 2,107 were women. This represents a mild increase from corresponding statistics for 1982, which show female representation of 21.5 per cent for *tokudo* and 7.1 per cent for *kyoshi* ordination. Women and men undertake ordination training together, have the same duties, and are required to pass the same exams. While the number of resident temple ministers who are men has decreased from 9,038 in 1982 to 8,930 in 2002, the opposite is true for women. There are currently 246 female resident ministers in Japan, compared to 129 in 1982. One must keep in mind that from the mother temple in Kyoto down to the smallest temple in the countryside, the traditional system of designating the temple head has been through patrilineal inheritance. That this is beginning to change is a result of factors relating mainly to society and economics in Japan. As young men are choosing to leave temple homes in favour of more interesting or more lucrative employment, it is becoming more acceptable for daughters or wives to step in as *jūshoku* (resident minister).

Japanese people who aspire to study Shin Buddhism, whether or not in preparation for ordination, have equal access to the seminaries or universities without age or sex discrimination, as long as qualifications are met. Likewise, women or men may become ordained if requirements are fulfilled.[12] From my own experience as a student at one such seminary, women formed a significant portion of the student body and were actively encouraged to participate in special rituals and ceremonies, as well as in clubs practicing liturgy, classical instrumental temple music, and homiletics.

At the mother temple, however, women on the sizable administrative staff are generally accorded a lesser status than men, even though they may be ordained and have the same educational background. There were only two women in management as of 2002, out of more than forty positions at that level.[13]

Thus, women are no more impeded than men from attaining qualifications and becoming ordained as ministers if they so aspire. However, to become a *kaikyoshi* overseas minister is a different matter. This is a designation, not a mark of further training, which is conferred by the Hongwanji in consultation with the overseas districts. Some districts, such as Hawaii and South America, have histories of women in their ranks. Canada also expresses equal opportunity for women ministers and is very welcoming in its approach to any qualified person in terms of offering financial assistance for education and training. In all of these districts, as in the United States, the decision rests in the hands of the Bishop. In the BCA, the Bishop is elected by a committee consisting of an equal number of ministers and laity, and he is presumed to represent the interests of the national body.

In this section, I will investigate women's perceptions regarding female ministers. Are women willing to accept a female minister in their temple? The response was a resounding yes – of the 170 women who replied to this question, only two (Nisei, eighties; Sansei, seventies) answered in the negative, and they offered no reason. Five women, including these two, said that women should not be encouraged to become ministers, even though three of them would accept a woman minister. Of these three, one – a Nisei in her seventies – stated,

- A woman can serve better if she educates herself like a woman and does not try to act like a male minister.

Would this exclude the possibility of educating oneself as a female minister? The respondent did not elaborate. The remaining two (Issei, fifties; Sansei, sixties) felt that it was a matter of aspiration and individual choice, rather than one of "encouragement" and indicated support of any aspirant, male or female.

Indeed, many women commented that for a minister, there were no particular advantages or disadvantages to being either male or female since ability, attributes, and knowledge are not determined by gender or sex. Notable among this kind of remark were the following:

- Each person has their own personality and character whether they are male or female… either can have their shortcomings.
- No differentiation if competent and qualified. A female minister should be able to perform all the duties expected of a male. We should not go out specifically to recruit women.
- The important aspect is to be knowledgeable of Buddhism and present information in a sincere and interesting manner. Any minister who can communicate is good.
- Women can teach the truth as well as a male. The spreading of the teaching is all the same.
- They shouldn't be judged by gender but by their leadership.
- As men and women have differences in general and work in various professions, why should the ministry be different? Skill in propagation, communication, understanding, etc. aren't sex-related.

These comments are representative of perspectives from American society, in which looking at women or men as "people" has become a trend, and gender constructs are not expected to impinge on occupational ability or opportunity.

The responses to the youth survey were even more pronounced in indicating that the teenagers have been raised to accept equal ability and equal rights as a basic foundation of their society. Most of them commented to this effect and many sounded surprised that the question was even asked. One young lady transcended the gender point altogether and replied that women should be encouraged to become ministers because "I think it's a good job to have." Others also offered refreshing insights:

- Our country is encouraging of equal opportunities. [male/female respondent(s)]
- Because if Buddhism is equal to all sexes, then why not? [m/f]
- Because I believe in Jōdo Shinshū everyone is equal.

Some may feel female ministers may be more appealing. [m/f]

- So the church is not so sexist. [m/f]
- Because women can do anything. [f]
- More women should be leaders. [f]
- So there could be women in this job. Once there are more women, more will be encouraged to join. [f]
- Yes [women should be encouraged], because I've yet to see one. [m]
- She could relate better to females. [f]
- Women are just as good as men; perspectives on Buddhism should be told from both a man's and a woman's perspective. [m]
- Everyone should have the opportunity to become a minister. Single-gendered ministries, such as Catholicism, limit the peoples' view toward their religion. [m]
- Women's issues are important. [m]
- As long as they do a good job it's okay. [m]
- I think we should all have the same opportunity and either everyone or no one should be encouraged. [m]

In these responses, the generational difference in social thinking is indisputable. Presumably, the young people did not arrive at this attitude without input from their parents as well as the rest of their environment. Many of them indicated that their mothers had college or graduate-level educations and professional careers, which would be in keeping with the sociological profile of the Sansei. As noted in chapter two, the acculturation of Japanese Americans is well on its way to completion. That most BCA temples continue to show an ethnic face demonstrates that the assimilation process has not reached a definitive end, but in attitude and perspective there is little doubt that these members are American.

To return to the women, they offered a multitude of reasons for welcoming female ministers. Several cited the shortage of ministers, especially of ministers who could speak English. Some women noted that they could not comment because they had never met a woman minister.

However, other opinions shared could be categorized as follows:

- Equal opportunity, equal ability, equal aspiration
- Reflects the doctrine of equality.
- Role model, validates diversity, changes the perception of society, allows children to see temple as a non-male-dominant place and culture
- Previous positive experiences with women ministers
- Perceived attributes particular to women: good communicators, good listeners, caring, sincere, empathetic, sympathetic, nurturing, compassionate, patient, tolerant, understanding, sensitive, kinder, gentler, more personable, more open-minded, better teachers, more collaborative and consensus-oriented, better networkers; better organizational and strategic planning skills; have a toughness men don't have.
- More inclined to take personal risk. The concern for an individual is stronger than the unwritten "rules" of the temple.
- Different perspective, more intuitive connection
- Relates better on issues of marriage, family, children, women's issues, health etc.
- More involvement in social issues
- Could tie the dharma into daily life; women seem to understand change and are not so set in their ways.
- Men are still predominantly in the "made in Japan" mode. Women are more assimilated because they have to be.
- Would attract younger women and families and could help strengthen the BWA
- Easier to talk to, especially for children and women; could boost Dharma School
- Could counsel
- May start new traditions and may cause some men to interact differently – change is positive.

Many of the above points are not based on fact, but represent the perceptions and speculation of some of the women. Other members observed that men should be equally capable of performing the same functions or could exhibit similar qualities, just as women were equally capable of being leaders or could exhibit attributes normally associated with men. This echoes Lehman's research, cited in chapter two, in which he demonstrated that reality often belied perceptions of differences between male and female ministers.

Women were also asked if they believed there were any drawbacks to having a female minister. Again, the response was striking in its uniformity. The vast majority of comments related to concerns that older male members might have difficulty accepting a woman because they (men) were "too old-fashioned/macho/shy/chauvinistic/narrow-minded," or that men tended to act overbearing and superior and would try to dominate a woman minister without having the respect for her that they would accord a man. Some respondents generalized their concerns to "some older members," male or female, who might not feel comfortable with women in traditionally male roles, though the respondents themselves, regardless of age, were supportive. It would be informative to know what the individual "older members" who did not participate in this research really think. Is there a general trend, and if so, can it be categorized by generation, sex, or cultural orientation? Is this an unfounded perception?[14]

Some people anticipated that the resistance would come from ministers and not from congregants. They believed that women ministers would "face extra hardships in contending with male ministers who are insecure, insensitive, and unaccepting of female ministers." Others believed the women would have to prove themselves to gain respect, though this could be true of any new minister. One individual pointed out that in other professions, "women have to prove themselves two hundred per cent more, and there are always going to be guys who feel inadequate." However, another person remarked,

- She may have to deal with some members who will test her strength and abilities rather than just accept the person, which would possibly be the reception given to a male minister.

A woman in her forties ventured,

- It would be a tough life, harder than for a man.

On the practical side, there were concerns that a woman minister would have greater difficulties raising a family, though two members, speaking of maternity leave, both added that male ministers should be accorded family leave as well. On this note, a complaint often heard from male ministers is that their duties do not allow them sufficient time with their families. Reflecting developments in other professions, it is possible that the presence of enough women in the ministry will bring awareness of and provoke welcome change to certain aspects of the job – for example in consideration of the quality of life for the minister and his or her family. In American society, fathers are expected to share equally in parenting and most congregants demonstrate this. Though some male ministers may have voiced a desire for better family conditions, they inevitably get caught in traditional attitudes passed on to them by their senior colleagues.

According to Nesbitt, women should seek ordination only if they want to reinvent the ministry and make positive changes to the institution. Otherwise, she says, they are supporting unjust patriarchal structures by perpetuating outmoded definitions and expectations.[15] As noted in chapter two, however, women ministers do not generally become clones of male ministers and as surveyed members surmised, they actually contribute an added perspective not only to the teaching but also to the profession.

Moreover, it might be noted that some women who enter the ministry do not have children; others place their calling above the desire to have a family; and still others are entering second careers and may have adult children. Thus, it would be unfair to dismiss women based on the categorical presumption that they will be preoccupied with their own families, though this is still the prevailing attitude in Japan, where women are expected to retire from careers once they marry.[16]

One person also mentioned the difficulty of assigning a woman to an unsafe district where some of the temples are located, and others mentioned harassment problems. Unfortunately, violence and harassment can threaten any minister, male or female, and it is up to the organization to ensure that all possible measures and safeguards are put into place to prevent such events from occurring.

There were a few opinions expressed that a woman could "have a one-track mind or be catty/opinionated/aggressive/domineering/emotional and cater to certain groups." Thus, it is evident that stereotyping was not confined to men alone, and that it was not all positive for women. Ultimately, congregants would be well-advised to judge each minister on her or his individual merits, as each has different strengths and weaknesses.

## THOUGHTS AND EXPERIENCES OF WOMEN MINISTERS IN JŌDO SHINSHŪ

None of the female ministers I interviewed originally aspired to become a temple minister. Some were not raised in the Shin Buddhist tradition, yet all of them shared a common path of wanting to study Buddhism, and Jōdo Shinshū in particular, for themselves. In every case, this personal interest led other ministers and members to beseech them to enter the ministry. Most of the women were searching for acceptable philosophies or teachings that would guide them in life. One individual was repelled by the rigid doctrine of her childhood religion that did not connect with the reality of her circumstances; another felt that other traditions did not point her toward satisfactory answers. Two admired grandfathers who were dedicated to Buddhism; another grew up in a strong family tradition of participation in the Shin temple. Two were impressed early on by older immigrant women who were devout followers of Shinshū. Three also specifically noted that they were influenced by mentor-teachers who deepened their understanding, thereby drawing them in closer to their commitment.

None experienced barriers to ordination, though some said that discrimination was sometimes subtle and may not always have been related to gender. One recounted,

- Some of the ministers and some of the students gave me a kind of shunning, like I was invisible. It was okay because the balance was on the positive side by far.

If there was discrimination, some said, it was because of race or of not being from a lineage (by birth) of ministers. One thought that being seen as coming from the community was an advantage.

None mentioned encountering any problems in their careers relating to the fact that they are women, though one sued the BCA over a case of sexual harassment about ten years ago, arising from an incident involving a telephone call from a male colleague.[17] The case was eventually dismissed based on insufficient grounds. The plaintiff had never wanted the affair to go to litigation at all, but the organization had failed to take what she and many women members considered to be necessary remedial action. In the aftermath, as mentioned earlier, the BCA did implement a sexual harassment policy. One woman lay leader believed that this resulted in making ministers very aware of gender issues and "even if they aren't completely women-oriented, they aren't going to say anything." Another mentioned that when the incident occurred, she was already cognizant of experiences other women had had with male ministers who made lewd suggestions and remarks with improper sexual overtones, but that it reached a limit for her to see a woman minister treated with such disrespect. In her opinion, it was important to pursue the issue, and she explained why:

- It won't be so easy the next time for this kind of thing to happen – not just the incident, but our ignoring it. The organization has to be responsive to problems of that nature and not push it aside as they did.

Another leader felt that the atmosphere was changing for the better, but that training had to be kept up.

All of the ministers, including the one in question, said they were focused on studying and teaching the dharma, and ministering to their members. In this sense, what they do fits with the women's perceptions of the duties of a minister, though there was some equivocation about the extent of the social aspects of the job. One of the ministers declared that she has been treated equally, in that she has been both mistreated and treated well, just like the men. There was no problem with equal compensation or opportunities.

Asked if they perceived any advantages to being a woman in this calling, some said that women and children related easily to them. A couple of them said that being older gave a warm maternal image that some members responded to, while another person said that having nurturing and listening qualities helped. For example, women approach them on marriage and family matters. Another opinion held that women would also be excellent in pastoral counseling and the chaplaincy. On the other hand, some of the ministers also remarked that people had a tendency to stereotype the maternal image and assume (as the surveys show) that they should be more involved with counseling, with children and youth in Dharma School, and other activities, even though they may not even have children of their own. In chapter two, it was noted that in other religious traditions in America, clergywomen risked being "ghettoized" in certain roles, such as those involving children. One of the ministers stated that while she was happy to teach children, she was fully qualified to talk to adults, too. In terms of being respected, it was also mentioned that there was an advantage to being older, and a second-career person.

Some of the ministers felt that the content, design, and delivery of female ministers' talks might connect more naturally with women. One explained,

- As women, we use very concrete examples from our lives, from the lives around us. When you hear a man, the stories that they share are not really about their own life but about something they may have heard. They give very good descriptions in terms of Rennyo's life, Shinran's life, Kakunyo's life, but not their own life. We [women] choose to speak about the issues of life that we struggle with and the relationship of our struggles and our insights based on the realization of some the teachings. So we come from life into the teachings, whereas our male counterparts go from teachings to "why." Think about how a male would prepare for a *fujinkai* conference.

One person did point out that a woman does not necessarily have to deal with the Old Boy games that the male ministers automatically slip into, or participate in group activities they don't always enjoy. On the other hand,

- If you want to be taken seriously all the time, it isn't going to happen. You have to find other ways to get your point across. Success depends on your personality, not your education.

Another stated that she picked her battles carefully and made her point quick and strong. She explained,

- The men do not like the women to be too verbal as that is like the negative aspect of a wife to them.

The observation was made that women could fall into a trap of feeling unappreciated or disrespected, thus holding on to resentful feelings instead of letting them go.

According to these ministers, whether a male minister is sexist or not is a matter of personal predilection rather than a result of nationality or age. Some of the older Japanese ministers are striving hard to be egalitarian, while some of the Sansei males "make an attempt to be like Meiji ministers." One of the women also remarked that some Caucasian male ministers "are perceived by members as thinking they are special and that members are lower than they." On Japanese ministers, one speculated that perhaps they were not used to having female colleagues in Japan, and simply did not know how to react.

Regarding the attitudes of laymen toward women ministers,

- They are respectful up to a point but on a national level politically, because you are a woman, they will not hear you. Sometimes you need to have someone present an issue for you because [echoing the previous remark of another minister about male ministers] of the way they don't listen to their own wives.

At the temple level, it was agreed that attitudes varied drastically from one place to another, depending on how culturally Japanese the majority of the members were, as well as their average age, the size of the community, and whether it was urban or rural. One individual reported that some elders, male and female, missed the sound of the male chanting and male delivery of a *howa* [sermon].

The ministers knew what the members expected of them, as listed earlier in this chapter. With regards to the duties directly involving the dharma, they were in accord. One stated,

- I am there in the service of our members for their faith, development, growth … in terms of serving them through Jōdo Shinshū. I'm with them in the process, enquiring with them, examining with them, not necessarily as if I have the answers.

One minister noticed that women seemed to show more interest in learning the dharma than men, yet at the same time, the *fujinkai* often missed dharma talks because they were busy in the kitchen and young mothers were preoccupied with watching their children in the temple.

On other expectations expressed by members, they pointed out the realistic side of personality, and human capability in terms of time and energy, both of which limit any minister, male or female. Further, regarding some members who want the minister to support the ethnic, cultural, and sports traditions, one replied,

- It's their identity. It's not the minister's ideal role. Some Japanese Americans are desperately clinging to tradition and culture, and the church is the last bastion of Japaneseness. But the religious activities get pushed way to the side of the social and cultural activities.

Still, what the ministers all said they enjoyed about their work was the people. They liked sharing with them in the process of learning about the self and finding a way through life by applying the doctrine in a safe environment that they provided.

What helped them to cope, especially in a male-dominated environment?

- A sense of humour.
- You have to be clear about yourself and comfortable with what you are doing.
- Have the courage to be yourself, informed by compassion and wisdom.
- Know how to bend.

One minister declared,

- Women see things in a less combative way. Working together is a stronger female trait, not that men can't do this. Women will compromise to the point where everyone will have something, rather than all for one. Men get locked into winning. It's negative because it destroys their ability to be effective if they win too many times. Shinshū is under-appreciated for its value of constantly putting you in touch with having to face down your ego. If you don't pay attention to this, you lose.

She did allow this concession:

- Some ministers need to have a strong ego because some lay people are sometimes brutal about the way they see the minister as an employee.

I asked whether they thought that Jōdo Shinshū would be attractive to mainstream Americans. An attraction, they replied, was that the temples stressed the family aspect, and the doctrine was practiced in daily life so that everyone was working together to support each other. One minister ventured that the doctrine would be useful to people in mainstream America, explaining,

- It helps you to accept life as it comes through the self-reflective mode. A lot of people appreciate this, women especially because we get all these messages that we have to make everyone happy, doing this and that for others. Women really appreciate the more "organic" approach of Shinshū, as opposed to a more disciplined, programmatic practice. You come here with your issues and we talk about why they bother you.

But another believed that it would be difficult to attract people who were approaching Buddhism for the first time because they were possibly looking for something different, such as meditation, rather than what they were used to.

- However, having had the initial exposure to Buddhism, they may be drawn to Jōdo Shinshū later because they experience the difficulties of attaining through meditative practice, unless they find a monastery that is going to take care of all their worldly needs.

She went on to posit,

- If Jōdo Shinshū is offered in the sense of being a lay Buddhist tradition and we are able to get it out of the fairy tale presentation of "Just say the Buddha's Name and he is going to save you," then we have more of a chance of appealing to Americans because they're very intellectual in that way. They don't want a fairy tale. They can go to Christian churches and get that.

However, one frankly observed,

- It also depends on the minister and how capable they are of answering questions. Some cannot deal with it.

# ON THE FUTURE OF JŌDO SHINSHŪ IN AMERICA

All of the women saw the ethnic dimension of the institution as an obstacle to sharing the teaching in America. Declared one minister,

- The future of Jōdo Shinshū in America is guaranteed only if the Institute of Buddhist Studies stays vibrant.[18] It is not ethnocentric. Also, the temples have to change before they will be comfortable to non-Asians.

Another noted that right now,

- People have to like Japanese culture and be rather intellectual because it is not an easy teaching. On the other hand, it isn't black and white.

And a third advocated,

- A parallel organization of people who are only interested in the dharma and not necessarily in the Japanese culture because we're in a situation where if we get new members we almost have to teach them to be Japanese in order to be able to participate in all the activities and fit in seamlessly.

One of the ministers took stock of the hierarchical form of the institution that is so distant from Shinran's lay ministry. She speculated,

- If we set up a purpose, form will follow, and check your ego at the door. Jōdo Shinshū will continue as long as people come to hear the teachings. The form, the institution, may not be as vital. Look at Europe and Alaska. They went ahead and brought together people who wanted to hear the teachings and impacted their lives without this institution. So the center that holds them is the teaching and not all of the other trappings. Maybe over time

we re going to see a way of decentralizing the institution
for good or bad.

But she conceded that there was a catch, in that while the institution
focused too much on membership, membership was needed to support
programs. Still, she said,

- We should look at the kind of programs and services we
  offer, not how many people become members.

Another minister agreed. Regarding the growth of Shinshu, she
predicted,

- It is not going to be leaps and bounds in our lifetime, and
  that s not a bad thing. If we concentrate on the deepening
  process of each of us trying to learn about it and share it
  with others, in the long run, people will appreciate that
  we did that. The social reason for coming to the temple
  is going away. The younger people don t feel that they
  have to go to a Japanese church anymore. Now we can
  concentrate on the people who want to hear the message
  and people in Shinsh temples should accept the fact that
  we are not going to have a big crowd. People don t need
  to go to a temple for sports or as a community center.

Yet another one pointed out that it was a people issue, not an organizational issue.

Finally, one admonished,

- We live in America. It s our advantage; we should be
  experimenting. They have to follow tradition in Japan,
  we don t. As a Buddhist you should be responding to
  your situation, not perpetuating any strange Japanese
  customs that have no touch with your reality. Our advantage is that we can speak to members in their own
  idiom, to their needs. We don t start talking about it from
  a *Dharmak ya* point of view. We haven t learned how to
  do it skillfully yet.

Certainly, the change of venue presents exciting possibilities for
Buddhism, in keeping with the transformations that have accompa-
nied its progress through many societies, cultures and ages. One thing

that would help the process is to encourage a diversity of people into the ministry. On attracting the young, one minister ventured,

- The image of ministers is that you have to be old and speak Japanese. None of the young people get excited, whereas if they can get excited about the teachings and can see that you don t have to be a clone...

In this vein, some of the interviewees noted the importance of having a variety of role models to demonstrate that ministers were not all cut of the same cloth. Indeed, as the responses to the youth surveys showed, positive role models in this area were clearly lacking. While twelve young men indicated that they would consider the ministry as a career, only two young women did the same, and one of them, a fourteen-year-old Yonsei asked,

- Are there women reverends?

The other said she was interested because she found that the teaching had helped her through "rough times." She wanted to spread the teachings to help others as it helped her.

Most teenagers, however, did not find the ministry appealing. Mainly, they had no interest in it, they had other plans, or they felt that they weren t religious enough. The young men, however, listed other reasons that primarily had to do with the perceived difficulties of the job: very time consuming, too hard, seems boring, not enough pay. One summed it up by saying, "I hear it s not the best job." On the other hand, their female counterparts did not look at the profession itself, but at their own capabilities:

- I value the teachings, but do not like speaking in front of other people.
- I think it would be interesting to study, but I m not sure I would want to lead.
- I m not that good at teaching. I d rather listen than teach.
- I probably wouldn t be good at it.
- I m not patient enough.
- Being a minister puts you in a high position in a community. I doubt I d be able to handle that.

- Usually they are men and I don't think I am that dedicated and understanding of religion.

The stark difference in perspective raises a number of questions. What is the link with socio-cultural upbringing? What role do religious teachings emphasizing humility play, and does this affect women more than men? Much research has been conducted on self-image differences based on sex. One such ethnically-based study published in 1974 by Larry Onoda compared Japanese American Sanseis. He reported:

> Males had a higher motivation to achieve as self-report-
> ed than the females, but the females were more likely to be
> high-achievers. There were no significant differences in actu-
> al GPA's, achievement scores, or intelligence scores between
> males and females.[19]

It would be useful to have similar research conducted today on the children of his subjects' generation, and an investigation into the causes of the differences in perception and orientation. One possible factor is the absence of female role models to validate the aspirations and achievements of young women, and to give them a sense of empowerment about their abilities. The lack of women in leadership positions also has a subtle influence on perceptions of both males and females with regard to equality.

One of the laywomen interviewed told me,

- The first woman *sensei* I knew was Rev. Okahashi (served 1966–1974). I thought she was so wonderful, at that time I thought, "I want to go into the ministry," and seriously considered it several times over the years. I thought she was great, a unique person, the first one I ever came across... she was a role model.

This person ultimately chose not to go into the ministry for undisclosed reasons. Another Sansei told me that it did not occur to her that women could be ministers because when she was growing up, she didn't see any. As a Dharma School teacher, she tries "to encourage the guys to be Dharma School teachers so the little guys will see that it's okay for guys to be involved in Dharma School."

One of the female lay leaders stressed,

- The selection of ministers should include lay people because the ministers will be serving them. If only ministers
  choose, they will always choose people like themselves.
  We will never progress if we continue with the same kind
  of people. We see the results of that. Young people are
  leaving; they go to their partners' religion.

Clearly, the ministry plays a decisive role in the future of Jōdo Shinshū
in America. From the interviews, women ministers demonstrated their
understanding of the challenges and their concern for sharing the teaching
with others. Members indicated that the way ministers related to them was
paramount. The inclination of respondents is to see a deepening of the
relationship. Not only do they want to be able to understand the dharma
from the ministers, but they also expect to see the ministers exemplify
attitudes of open-mindedness, equality, and undiscriminating care for
every member.

Not all of the issues were gender-related. Much of the tension, as
Mullins theorized, has been brought about by generational change in a
rapidly acculturating ethnic environment. This has resulted in an irreversible
transformation of social and cultural expectations which the institution –
including the ministers – is now facing. One of the indicators of apposite
change undoubtedly will be in the way that ministers are perceived to
view women, both as colleagues and as congregants. As one of the women
stated, cooperation is the key to making this work for everyone.

# CONCLUSION

From the beginning, the participation of women in Buddhism has always been hampered by the limitation of gender constructs imposed on them by their Asian societies. Today in America, those limitations are loosening in a mainstream society that is being transformed by developments as wide-ranging as democratization, pluralism, and feminism. It would seem the perfect environment for the flowering of a Buddhist doctrine which professes non-discrimination and universal application. Indeed, scholars and adherents now speak of "American Buddhisms" that have attributes reflective of their new progressive surroundings. Yet excluded from this phenomenon have been the various schools of ethnic Buddhism, considered too Asian to suit Americans. Counted among these is Japanese Jōdo Shinshū which, although it has been in this country for five generations, still resists adaptation. Listening to the voices of the women featured, there is little doubt that they consider themselves American, and that they want to relate to their doctrine as such.

Over a century ago, Jōdo Shin Buddhism came West when Japan ended its long isolation from the rest of the world. Japanese immigrants, the first generation Issei, brought with them not only their religion, but also their patriarchal values of the Meiji era. Not long afterwards, the Oriental Exclusion Act came into effect, followed by further discrimination during the war years with "evacuation" and internment camps. The community, by then augmented by American-born second generation Nisei, drew closer together in ethnic unity. The most conservative bastion of the community, the Buddhist temple, signified for many a link with their cultural heritage, and thus perpetuated the Japanese character of the institution.

As Mullins pointed out in chapter two, the goal of the ethnic church often plays a major role in the preservation of customs, language, and group solidarity for the first generation. But as subsequent generations acculturate, the institution must adapt and reorient its goals or risk extinction. Third generation Sansei women came of age along with the sweeping social transformations in mainstream society. Yet according to research respondents, the institution has not kept up with the times, the culture outside of the temple, or the needs of its members. Many express ambivalence about the existing institution to the extent that they are concerned about the future of Jōdo Shinshū in America. They desire that the religion be made understandable, relevant, and vibrant for today's membership. This is the main focus of attention, to which social and cultural activities would be secondary. In order to fulfill this objective, they see a need for ministers who can relate to them as Americans, and a temple environment that is representative of what they accept and laud as a doctrine of equality for all people.

For the first time in history, perhaps, prevailing social values and the tenets of Buddhism are more in accord on the subject of non-discrimination. Yet within the BCA organization, women still notice a male-dominant attitude on the part of some ministers and some elders – an attitude that starkly contrasts with the outlook of today's youth, who have been raised on the principle of equality and unlimited possibility, regardless of sex, race, or other distinctions. Some respondents venture that if the temple and the teaching are not made more relevant to everyone, the rapid attrition in membership that started a few decades ago will continue unabated.

Have the goals of the organization changed? One hundred years ago, devout immigrants requested that ministers be sent from Japan to serve their religious needs. Many members can still recount stories of mothers and grandmothers who lived daily in the Jōdo Shin teaching. In the circumstances of their day, the Issei also came to see the temple as an ethnic gathering place. The events of modern history sustained this focus and prolonged it beyond their own generation. Perhaps due to the dearth of ministers who could truly communicate and relate well to later generations, the religious underpinning of the institution has lost much of its meaning for today's members, and the temple often seems to be held together by other activities. Yet despite, or perhaps because of this trend, it is striking that so many women of all generations voice the need to bring religion back as the central aim. What is significant is that they express an opinion that the Jōdo

Shin doctrine is still viable and valuable to them. If they know about the thirty-fifth vow at all, it is a non-issue to them in this day and age as they focus on the principal import of the doctrine, that of universal liberation. Accordingly, they add, the Shin Buddhist teaching should also be made available to other people outside of the ethnic enclave. Some of them speak from the experience of what the teaching means in their own spiritual search; others articulate hopes that what is intimated about this path will be clarified and demonstrated in more engaging terms. Female converts have added their voices to this, indicating a very real opportunity to share Jōdo Shinshū with the wider community.

If male-dominant attitudes are an obstacle, the women are proving that they have been able to transcend them without stridency, simply by being who they are – American Buddhists raised to know that the worth of all beings is equal. This does not mean that they want to be the same as the men, nor that they aspire to replace them as the group in power. Instead, they see themselves as working together effectively with the men by contributing their considerable insight, intelligence, and skills in leadership to create a religious institution that will serve everyone more effectively. Knowing what it is to be marginalized may also afford them an informed view of broader issues of access which are so important to the future of Jōdo Shinshū in America.

Related to this is the realization that young people need to see that this religion is relevant to the diversity of the world in which they live, both through the issues it addresses and the impression it gives. Their typical image of a minister is an older man who speaks Japanese and performs funerals and memorial services. This may be the accepted norm in Japan, but it is hardly inspiring for Americans, as demonstrated by the research responses. Yet here too the difference can be viewed as an opportunity. For while routinization of the tradition may have become entrenched in Japan, the respondents feel it is not too late to recognize that Jōdo Shinshū now finds itself in a completely new environment that is conducive to positive change. Their optimism and enthusiasm toward the survey clearly suggest that the possibility exists to revalorize the teaching and interpret it in new ways that speak to contemporary people not only in America, but everywhere. This is not without precedent. Hōnen and Shinran went through a similar process in their time, departing from Indian and Chinese traditions to create a Japanese Buddhism that worked for them and for their contemporaries.

Obviously, many related issues have arisen out of this examination of women in American Jōdo Shinshū today. It has been useful and instructive to ask the women to share their views, for though they may not always have been at the head of the temple, they have always been at the center. They can accurately identify problems that exist and offer concrete suggestions that address the long-term needs of the congregation. Gender issues are not the only problem, but they are indicative of the enormous chasm that has grown between the majority of the American sangha and the patriarchal culture of the old country. Indeed, the inevitable acculturation of those in leadership, both male and female, will undoubtedly mitigate discriminatory tensions in the laity. However, it is also important that the ministry understand and adapt, if necessary, to differences in socio-cultural viewpoint. Without this, there might soon be no listeners to hear them. It must be emphasized that there have been a number of ministers, both Japanese and American, who have done much to reach out to congregants and to make the teaching relevant to them. However, judging by the comments of the women interviewed, there are not enough ministers in the system with a diversity of perspective, or attitudes conducive to suitably transmitting the dharma here. Admittedly, there are members who are comfortable with current conditions, and respondents agree that those people should continue to be served in a manner that suits them. But will younger members who remain with the BCA receive a religious education appropriate to their needs? And what of the droves of disenchanted Buddhists who are leaving the organization to seek religion elsewhere – or who have simply become disillusioned by religion altogether?

For many reasons, relatively few young Americans are called to the ministry, and this applies to the Shin Buddhist ministry as well. Without role models with whom they can identify, then, it is difficult for Shinshū followers to find the necessary motivation, even if they can overcome the other factors responsible for the decline in the ministry. Japanese ministers who sincerely wish to share the teaching are greatly appreciated, but their training, say the women, must go beyond learning rudimentary English. It is also necessary that they learn about American society and its cultural values so that they can relate to congregants in a suitable manner. Further, they need to be educated in America, and particularly in areas that congregants identify with the ministry, such as counseling and social outreach. Moreover, women should not be barred from the ministry if they are qualified. Respondents gave ample reasons to show that the inclusion of female ministers would benefit everyone. Notably, they would add another perspective to what has been an almost exclusively androcentric orientation. The only barrier, it seems, has been the discriminatory stance of some people, which has then fostered an attitude that women cannot be ministers.

Some of the women made a clear distinction between their faith in the teaching and their trepidation about the institution. In the past decade, more women have begun to push for change by taking leadership roles. Does their presence create holes in the fabric of the institution? Perhaps it does from a traditional point of view, although the transition appears to have been both timely and natural. In any event, the case at hand demonstrates that the BCA needs to be fluid and flexible, as several members question what they call lack of relevance and vision. Therefore, the inclusion of women on a level of parity could be viewed positively as a welcome change, rather than as a threat, that may shake the organization out of its lassitude and bring in new energy.

It is telling that some women are willing to pursue Jōdo Shinshū with or without the institution of the BCA. Some speak of smaller *howakai* study groups and others speak of parallel organizations for people who are not interested in Japanese culture but simply want to study Shin Buddhism. In fact, recently installed Bishop Koshin Ogui was already making innovative adaptations to meet the needs of the American sangha when he was serving as a minister in the Eastern District. While it remains to be seen how he will lead the national organization during this crucial time of cultural transition, the move to create parallel organizations reinforces the idea that in one way or another, change is inevitable. Whether the institution can embrace it or not is another question.

Women have always been a source of strength in the temple both for their active support and for their influence on younger generations, yet even today they are seldom asked for their views, much less listened to. Their responses to the surveys and interviews show that many of them are eager for change in both the institution and in the way they are perceived. Regardless of generation or age, what most share here contradicts the stereotype of the acquiescent Japanese woman who kowtows to men.

A number of respondents express displeasure with the traditional status quo and several are taking the initiative to demonstrate capabilities that appear, until recently, to have been ignored. They contribute many insights that stem from their women's experience, which some of them are now applying as they participate in temple and BCA leadership.

Future research could include a larger sampling of members to enable comparisons between various kinds of temples based on location, size, age of members, and cultural orientation. It would also be useful to undertake further research to determine the views of male members and of the clergy on the same topics, to verify differences between perception and reality and to balance the input gathered from the women. Ultimately, this could lead to better mutual understanding and a stronger sense of direction for all involved. Research involving former members would also enable the organization to address problems and deficiencies.

What do these findings portend for the future? Since they appear to represent a wide, and sometimes contradictory range of opinions, it is difficult to forecast what lies ahead. The negative view might say that the BCA as a religious institution will have run its course if it cannot accommodate the changed profile of its members. Would Jōdo Shinshū be able to survive in America without this structure? From the creative responses of the women surveyed, it seems as if it would, at least in spirit. Women might even be the ones to lead the way, accustomed as they are to adjusting to changing circumstances.

Listening to many of those who contributed to this research, the hope for the future lies in focusing on religion rather than on ethnic culture. Such a move could change the direction of Jōdo Shinshū in America, but would require that greater efforts be made to adapt the dissemination of the religion to serve all generations as well as non-ethnics. For women, it would mean that gender issues might finally be put to rest as the organization becomes more mainstream.

Throughout its history, Buddhism has influenced society, and society in turn has influenced the development of the doctrine and the institution. As it traveled eastward through various cultures and societies, the dharma has taken root by harmonizing where fitting or necessary with the social environment. Along with the progress of Buddhism, women have often played a key role in fostering the mass appeal of the tradition through their own dedication and devotion. Now Buddhism has arrived in a social environment where women are much less limited by gender constructs. They are free to explore a new sense of self both in their worldly lives and on the level of Ultimate Reality, and Shinran's doctrine offers one possible path in this quest.

In Jōdo Shinshū the word *fukashigi* describes the inconceivable working of Amida Buddha that is beyond conceptual understanding. It seems like an appropriate term to apply to the remarkable confluence of Buddhism, feminism, pluralism, egalitarianism, and the acculturation of Jōdo Shin Buddhists in America. Perhaps beyond all human conditioning and calculation, Shin Buddhism, too, will transcend its bounds.

# ENDNOTES

## NOTES TO INTRODUCTION

1 Though there are ten independent schools of Jōdo Shin Buddhism in Japan, I refer in this work to the largest of the ten schools, also known commonly as Nishi Hongwanji or simply the Hongwanji. It is to this organization that the Buddhist Churches of America is affiliated.

2 Christopher Queen referring to studies by James Coleman, Phillip Hammond and David Machacek, introduction to Duncan Williams and Christopher Queen, eds., *American Buddhism: Methods and Findings* (Surrey: Curzon Press, 1999), xiv.

3 Charles Prebish, *Luminous Passage: The Practice and Study of Buddhism in America* (Berkeley, Los Angeles and London: University of California Press, 1999), 264, quoting Lama Surya Das in a presentation at the Buddhism in America Conference, Boston, 17–19 January, 1997.

4 For a detailed discussion of problems facing the BCA, see Alfred Bloom, "Shin Buddhism in America," in *The Faces of Buddhism in America*, ed. Charles S. Prebish and Kenneth K. Tanaka (Berkeley and Los Angeles: University of California Press, 1998), 40–46. Primary reasons cited by Bloom include outmarriage; problems related to the ministry (including language and cultural difficulties faced by Japanese ministers, and difficulties recruiting American youth due to conditions and lack of appeal); lack of activities for other than traditional nuclear families; lack of dynamic leadership; acculturation of younger generations; tensions between cultural and religious focus; inadequate religious education in the sangha; lack of outreach; misconceptions of outsiders regarding doctrine; and failure to be attractive to newcomers.

5 Sangha, Skt., lit. "crowd, host," originally consisted of monks, nuns, and novices. Later, in some schools of Buddhism, including Jōdo Shinshū, the sangha also came to include lay followers.

6 This will also affect views about women in the priesthood and clergy.

7 For example, the appeal to the masses of the Kamakura "new schools," including Shin Buddhism, broke the exclusive hold that Japanese

nobility and monasticism had on the religion, as will be explained in chapter one. Later, routinization of the institution, explained in chapter two, created both an elitist hierarchy and stagnation, which failed to reflect the fluidity of society and the truth of change. It is further noted that women can become marginalized in this process. In chapters three through five, women call for renewed relevance of the teaching to their everyday lives, without which some fear the institution may continue to lose members at considerable rates.

8  Karma Lekshe Tsomo, *Buddhist Women Across Cultures: Realizations* (Albany: State University of New York Press, 1999), 28–29.

## NOTES TO CHAPTER ONE

1  I.B. Horner, foreword to Diana Y. Paul, *Women in Buddhism: Images of the Feminine in Mahāyāna Tradition* (Berkeley: University of California Press, 1985), xv.

2  Diana Y. Paul, *Women in Buddhism: Images of the Feminine in Mahāyāna Tradition* (Berkeley: University of California Press, 1985), xix.

3  Ibid., xxiv–xxv.

4  Alan Sponberg, "Attitudes Toward Women and the Feminine in Early Buddhism," in *Buddhism, Sexuality and Gender*, ed. Jose Ignacio Cabezon (Albany: State University of New York Press, 1992), 8–28.

5  Diana Paul, *Images*; Susan Murcott, *The First Buddhist Women: Translation and Commentaries on the Therīgatha* (Berkeley: Parallax Press, 1991); Nancy Falk, "The Case of the Vanishing Nuns: The Fruits of Ambivalence in Ancient Indian Buddhism," in *Unspoken Worlds: Women's Religious Lives in Non-Western Cultures*, ed. Nancy A. Falk and Rita M. Gross (San Francisco: Harper and Row, 1979), 207–224.

6  Richard Gombrich, *Theravāda Buddhism: A Social History from Ancient Benares to Modern Colombo* (London: Routledge and Kegan Paul, 1988).

7  I.B. Horner, *Women Under Primitive Buddhism* (London: Routledge and Kegan Paul Ltd., 1930; reprint, Delhi: Motilal Barnasidass, 1975).

8  Karma Lekshe Tsomo, *Buddhist Women Across Cultures: Realizations* (Albany: State University of New York Press, 1999); Rita Gross, *Buddhism After Patriarchy: A Feminist History, Analysis, and Reconstruction of Buddhism*. Albany: State University of New York Press, 1993).

9 I.B. Horner, 82 (page citation is to the reprint edition).

10 Jonathan Walters, "A Voice from the Silence: The Buddha's Mother's Story," in *History of Religions* (Chicago) 33, no. 4 (1994).

11 Sponberg, 4.

12 This opinion of Caroline Foley Rhys Davids and Mabel Bode is outlined in Walters, 359.

13 In fact, many of the rules and regulations for the communal life of monks and nuns (*Vinaya-pitaka*) were laid down so practitioners would stay within social boundaries and avoid social censure.

14 Horner, 95 ff.; Paul, 80ff.

15 That men no longer had to wait until retirement to enter the sangha, but could choose it over worldly pursuits was transgressive in itself. Perhaps it would have been too radical to allow women such a choice.

16 Charles Prebish, *Luminous Passage: The Practice and Study of Buddhism in America* ( Berkeley: University of California Press, 1999), 75.

17 For a description of epigraphical findings relating to nuns, see Gregory Schopen, *Bones, Stones, and Buddhist Monks; Collected Papers on the Archaeology, Epigraphy, and Texts of Monastic Buddhism in India.* (Honolulu: University of Hawaii Press, 1997), 64.

18 Janis Willis, "Nuns and Benefactresses: The Role of Women in the Development of Buddhism," in *Women, Religion, and Social Change*, ed. Yvonne Yazbeck Haddad and Ellison Banks Findly (Albany: State University of New York Press, 1985), 73.

19 *Sigalovadasutta*, verse 30, quoted in I.B. Horner, 41–42, says that "the husband should treat his wife with respect, courtesy and faithfulness, hand over authority to her and provide her with adornments; and that the wife should love her husband, perform her duties well, look after kin, be faithful, guard his wealth and manage servants and home with skill and industry."

20 For a study and analysis of the lives of early nuns and how the scriptures portrayed them, see Nancy Auer Falk, "The Case of the Vanishing Nuns: The Fruits of Ambivalence in Ancient Indian Buddhism," in *Women's Religious Lives in Non-Western Cultures*, ed. Nancy A Falk and Rita Gross (San Francisco: Harper and Row, 1979), 207–224.

21 Willis, 77.

22 Anne Bancroft, "Women in Buddhism," in *Women in the World's*

*Religions*, ed. Ursula King (New York: Paragon House, 1987), 86, says that evidence of this surfaces in the first century B.C.E., some four hundred years after the Buddha's death, when the Pali canon was first recorded in writing by scholarly monks who depicted women as obstacles to the liberation of monks.

23  Nancy Schuster Barnes, "Buddhism" in *Women in World Religions*, ed. Arvind Sharma (Albany: State University of New York Press, 1987), 118.

24  For a discussion of Weber's theory of "routinization" relating to this, see chapter two.

25  Nancy Barnes disputes the notion that such scriptures and practices were misogynistic, arguing that renunciants were relying on *upāya*, skillful means, to overcome their own sexuality. Nancy Barnes, "Buddhism," in *Women in World Religions*, ed. Arvind Sharma (Albany: State University of New York Press, 1987), 110–114. There were two trends in monastic Buddhism: one that saw the mind as the problem, and another that perceived the "other" as the problem.

26  Paul, 303.

27  However, the *Gandavyūha Sutra*, the final book of the *Avatamsaka Sutra*, believed to have been written in the second or third century C.E., appears to fit into this category. Some twenty of the fifty-three bodhisattva teachers are female figures but like all of the archetypes in the sutra, their incarnations are clearly provisional and not ultimately real. It is noteworthy that this sutra may have been contemporaneous with the *Sukhāvatīvyūha Sutra* which is the primary sutra of Jōdo Shin Buddhism and contains the 35th Vow, known as the "The Aspiration to Change from Female to Male," which will be discussed later. The *Prajñā-pāramitā Sutras* might also fall into this classification, though these are believed to have been composed over a span of centuries from 100 B.C.E. to the thirteenth century C.E.

28  For an analysis of scriptures of this variety, see Ho-Ryeon Jeon, "Can Women Achieve Enlightenment? A Critique of Sexual Transformation For Enlightenment," in *Buddhist Women Across Cultures*, ed. Karma Lekshe Tsomo (Albany: State University of New York Press, 1999), 123–141.

29  Sponberg, 25.

30  Ibid., 11.

31  Paul, xxvii.

32  For example, it is known that Prince Shotoku of Japan (574–622 C.E.) was an enthusiast of the *Vimalakīrti* and *Śrīmālā Sutras* which were

popular in China during his time. In 604 C.E. he proclaimed Buddhism as the state religion, yet these sutras did not seem to flourish, though they may have influenced Shinran and other masters of the new Kamakura schools some 600 years later. See Alex and Hideko Wayman, trans. *The Lion's Roar of Queen Śrīmālā: A Buddhist Scripture on the Tathāgatagarbha Theory.* (New York and London: Columbia University Press, 1974), 13–15.

33 *cakravartin*, Skt., lit. "wheel ruler;" a world ruler. It later became an epithet for a Buddha whose teaching is universal.

34 The last involve cases of female property and dowry rights, which indicate that women had more independence than the patriarchal society of the day suggests. For a detailed studies on women in Sung society, see works by Patricia Ebrey, Bettine Birge, and Kathryn Bernhardt, noted in the bibliography.

35 Alan Cole, *Mothers and Sons in Chinese Buddhism* (Stanford: Stanford University Press, 1998), 1–13.

36 Ibid., 80–102. The story of Mu Lian continues to be popular among Shin Buddhist followers in America today, although it is not a part of Jōdo Shinshū doctrine and, unlike adherents to some schools of Buddhism, Shin Buddhists do not purchase merit.

37 Viewed in another way, it must be remembered that the tendency in Buddha-dharma is towards non-discrimination and liberation. Concessions are made to social and cultural convention as expedient means (*upāya*) but are never meant to become regressive.

38 For a comprehensive study on this topic, see Chün-fang Yü, *Kuan-yin: The Chinese Transformation of Avalokiteśvara.* (New York: Columbia University Press, 2001).

39 For a summary of the history of nuns in Japan, see Akira Hirakawa, "The History of Buddhist Nuns in Japan," trans. Karma Lekshe Tsomo, *Buddhist-Christian Studies* 12 (1992): 147–158.

40 Bernard Faure, *The Power of Denial: Buddhism, Purity, and Gender.* (Princeton: Princeton University Press, 2003), 29.

41 Alicia and Daigan Matsunaga, *Foundation of Japanese Buddhism,* vol. 1 (Los Angeles and Tokyo: Buddhist Books International, 1974), 209.

42 Faure, 114. Given the developments in Ch'an Buddhism in China around the same period, this comment may refer to scriptures such as *The Blood Bowl Sutra* (Jp. *Ketsubongyo*) involving the story of Mu Lian and female menstrual defilement, mentioned earlier. These sutras were also made popular by monks in Japan. As for developments in the Ch'an school,

it is known that Dogen returned from study in China to exhort adherents to respect female teachers. See Miriam Levering, "Dogen's *Raihaitokuzui* and Women Teaching in Sung Ch'an," *Journal of the International Association of Buddhist Studies* 5, no. 1 (1988): 77–110.

43  Matsunaga and Matsunaga., vol. 2, 3.

44  Other well-known schools were Jodo, founded by Honen (1133–1212); Soto Zen, founded by Dogen (1200–1253); and Nichiren, founded by Nichiren (1222–1282), all offshoots of the Tendai school on Mt. Hiei near Kyoto.

45  Matsunaga and Matsunaga, vol. 2, 10.

46  "If, when I attain Buddhahood, sentient beings in the lands of the ten directions who sincerely and joyfully entrust themselves to me, desire to be born in my land, and call my Name even ten times, should not be born there, may I not attain perfect Enlightenment. Excluded, however, are those who commit the five gravest offences and abuse the right dharma." Translated by Hisao Inagaki, *The Three Pure Land Sutras*, 2d ed. (Kyoto: Nagata Bunshodo, 1995), 243. [TT. 12, 268a 26–28]

47  Dennis Hirota, Hisao Inagaki, Michio Tokunaga, and Ryushin Uryuzu, trans., *The Collected Works of Shinran,* Vol. 1, (Kyoto: Jodo Shinshu Hongwanji-ha, 1997), 107. (Hereafter referred to as CWS).

48  "If, when I attain Buddhahood, women in the immeasurable and inconceivable Buddha-lands of the ten directions who, having heard my Name, rejoice in Faith, awaken aspiration for Enlightenment and wish to renounce womanhood, should after death be reborn again as women, may I not attain perfect Enlightenment." Inagaki, trans., 246–247. [TT. 12, 268c21–24]

49  F. Max Muller, ed. and trans., *The Larger Sukhāvatīvyūha* (Sacred Books of the East, XLIX) (Oxford: Clarendon Press, 1894), 19; quoted in Diana Paul, 169–170.

50  For an examination of various versions of this vow in Sanskrit and Chinese, see Paul Harrison, "Women in the Pure Land: Some Reflections on the Textual Sources," *Journal of Indian Philosophy* 26, no. 6 (1998): 553–572.

51  Use of the word "faith" for the Japanese word shinjin is problematic in Jōdo Shinshū, but simply put, shinjin, unlike Protestant connotations, "denotes the central religious experience of Shin Buddhism, and literally means man's 'true, real, and sincere heart and mind,' which is given by Amida Buddha." CWS, Vol.2, 206.

52  Paul, 186.

53  For example, Nancy Barnes, noted earlier.

54  Bernard Faure posits that the Five Obstacles (women could not become a Brahma, Śakra, Māra, cakravartin king, or Buddha) was a political construct created by Theravādin monks and that it merged with traditional gender stereotypes to justify institutional submission of women and their exclusion from sacred places, or even from Buddhahood. He states that the Five Obstacles were originally a technical or juridical restriction that later came to be interpreted as ontological inferiority which in turn led to interpretations of karmic and moral inferiority, leading to female guilt. Faure, 62ff.

55  Recall the self-proclaimed status of Empress Wu, mentioned earlier.

56  This view is also supported by Haruko Okano in her essay on this topic, "Women's Image and Place in Japanese Buddhism," in *Japanese Women: New Feminist Perspectives on the Past, Present, and Future*, ed. Kumiko Fujimura-Fanselow and Atsuko Kameda (New York: The Feminist Press of The City University of New York, 1995), 15–28.

57  Haruko Okano states that the exclusion of women from Mt. Hiei was originally intended as part of monastic discipline and practice but that it resulted in giving additional power and authority to the temples.

Moreover, such sacred mountain temples "were closely connected with the ruling power, which looked to religion as a means of control." Okano, 22.

58  Ibid., 63–64 and 109.

59  Ibid., 65.

60  Ibid., 76.

61  Faure, citing the Kasahara theory. Ibid., 107.

62  CWS, Vol. 1, 107.

63  Okano, 23. She points out that such thinking on the part of the leaders of the new Kamakura religions has attracted critical attention of modern male researchers, making reference to Hajime Endo, "Bomori izen no koto," (The origin of marriage for priests of the Jōdo Shin Sect) in *Shinjin to kuyo* (*Faith and service for the dead*), ed. Osumi Kazuo et al. (Tokyo: Heibonsha, 1989).

64  Yoshiko Ohtani, *The Life of Eshinni: Wife of Shinran Shonin* , trans. Taitetsu Unno (Kyoto: Jodo Shinshu Hongwanji-ha, 1990) contains these letters with background.

65  With all due respect to Lady Ohtani, the wife of the twenty-third Abbot, one wonders why Hongwanji studies of its prominent women are

confined to those of *O-Urakata-Sama* (lit. "the person in the back," the Abbot's wife).

66 Masafumi Hata, lecture on Shin Buddhist history given in class on 11 January, 2002, at Chuo Bukkyo Gakuin, Kyoto.

67 Kakushinni's son was Kakue, the father of Kakunyō (1270–1351) who actually engineered the structure and lineage of the Hongwanji as it is today. Kakushinni had accepted the position as first caretaker of the memorial shrine and grounds, but she had agreed with followers that though each caretaker would appoint her or his successor, it would be subject to the approval of the followers, who financially supported both the memorial and Kakushinni. Her grandson, Kakunyō, usurped this trust and changed the role of caretaker to one of Abbotship. See James Dobbins, *Jōdo Shinshū in Medieval Japan* (Bloomington and Indianapolis: Indiana University Press, 1989), 80–83.

68 Like Kakushinni, Shinran had never envisaged a hereditary Abbotship as was instituted by Kakunyō. Shinran himself had disowned his eldest son, Zenran, over charges of heresy in 1256 and though he had other sons and daughters, it was Kakushinni who looked after him until his death.

69 As in Eshinni's case, the Hongwanji has no record of Kyojunni's dates.

70 Dobbins, 114–115.

71 Fascicle V, no. 20, translated by Minor Rogers and Ann Rogers, *Rennyo: The Second Founder of Shin Buddhism.* (Berkeley: Asian Humanities Press, 1991), 257.

72 Ohtani, 102. This opinion is shared by James Dobbins, "Women's Birth in the Pure Land as Women: Intimations from the Letters of Eshinni," *The Eastern Buddhist* 28, no. 1 (1995): 117–120.

73 The Meiji era lasted from 1868–1912.

74 Mioko Fujieda, "Japan's First Phase of Feminism," in Fujimura-Fanselow and Kameda, 323.

75 See Takeko Kujo, *Muyuge.* Los Angeles: The Nembutsu Press, 35.

76 Sponberg, 29.

# NOTES TO CHAPTER TWO

1 Nancy Schuster Barnes, "Buddhism" in *Women in World Religions*, ed. Arvind Sharma (Albany: State University of New York Press, 1987), 130–131.

2  For example, see Harry Kitano, *Generations and Identity: The Japanese Americans* (Needham Heights, MA: Ginn, 1993), 124 and 163; and Mei Nakano, *Japanese American Women: Three Generations 1890–1990* (Berkeley and Sebastopol: Mina Press Publishing, 1990), 225.

3  For a history of the BCA, see T. Kashima, *Buddhism in America: The Social Organization of an Ethnic Religious Institution* (Westport, CT: Greenwood Press, 1977); D. Tuck, *Buddhist Churches of America: Jodo Shinshu* (Lewiston and Queenston: The Edwin Mellen Press, 1987); and Buddhist Churches of America, *Buddhist Churches of America: A Legacy of the First Hundred Years* (San Francisco: Buddhist Churches of America, 1998).

4  Report of Kawai Michiko, "Fujin no Me ni Eizuru Tokō Fujin," *Nihon Imin Kyōkai Hōkoku*, no. 14, (3 December, 1917): 31–50, paraphrased in Yuji Ichioka, "*Amerika Nadeshiko*: Japanese Immigrant Women in the United States, 1900–1924," in *Ethnicity and Gender: The Immigrant Woman*, ed. George E. Pozzetta (New York and London: Garland Publishing, Inc., 1991), 112.

5  This was followed by the first World Buddhist Women's Convention of Jodo Shinshu Hongwanji-ha in 1961.

6  Tetsuden Kashima, *Buddhism in America: the Social Organization of an Ethnic Religious Institution*. (Westport, Ct.: Greenwood Press, 1977), 137–138.

7  Mei Nakano, *Japanese American Women: Three Generations 1890–1990*. (Berkeley and Sebastopol: Mina Press Publishing, 1990), 115.

8  Edna Bonacich and John Modell, *The Economic Basis of Ethnic Solidarity: Small Business in the Japanese American Community* (Berkeley, Los Angeles and London: University of California Press, 1980), 228.

9  Nakano, 106.

10  Ibid., 195–201.

11  Ibid., 208–210.

12  Robert Ito, "The Twenty-five Most Noteworthy Asians in America in 2001," *aMagazine* (December 2001/January 2002), 59.

13  Zen Lotus Society, "Chronology of Events Involving Women and Buddhism." *Women and Buddhism: A Special Issue of Spring Wind – Buddhist Cultural Forum* 6, no. 1, 2 & 3 (1986): 235–270.

14  While there are differences in size between the two organizations, the history of their members is similar. However, Canada does not have the concentrations of ethnic Japanese that can be found in some locations in

the United States. Such concentrations will further retard the assimilation process of some BCA temples. In any event, most temples of the BCC have not fully transformed in the way Mullins projected.

15  Mark Mullins, "The Life-Cycle of Ethnic Churches in Sociological Perspective," *Japanese Journal of Religious Studies* 14, no. 4 (1987): 322.

16  Ibid., 322–323.

17  Ibid., 324.

18  R. Stephen Warner and Judith G. Wittner, eds. *Gatherings in Diaspora: Religious Communities and the New Immigration* (Philadelphia: Temple University Press, 1998), 25.

19  Ibid., 325.

20  Essie E. Lee, *Nurturing Success: Successful Women of Color and Their Daughters* (Westport and London: Praeger Publishers, 2000), 134.

21  Nakano, 188.

22  Darrel Montero, *Japanese Americans: Changing Patterns of Ethnic Affiliation Over Three Generations* (Boulder, CO: Westview Press, 1980): 75, quoted in Mark Mullins, "The Organizational Dilemmas of Ethnic Churches: A Case Study of Japanese Buddhism in Canada," *Sociological Analysis* 49, no. 3 (1988): 227–228. In addition, Stephen S. Fugita and David J. O'Brien, *Japanese American Ethnicity: The Persistence of Community* (Seattle and London: University of Washington Press, 1991), 133–134, find that "the intermarried are less likely than the inmarried to attend an ethnic church."

23 Harry Kitano, "Interracial Marriage Rate Jumps in Each Genera-tion," *Asian Week*, 24 March, 1989, 15.

24  Dean S. Toji, "The Rise of a Nikkei Generation," in Dennis Arguelles and Eric Yo Ping Lai ed., *New Face of Asian Pacific America: Numbers, Diversity and Change in the 21st Century* (San Francisco: Asian Week with UCLA Asian American Studies Center Press, 2003), 77.

25  Hiro Nishimura, *Trials and Triumphs of the Nikkei* (Mercer Island, WA: Fukuda Publishers, 1993), 134.

26  Larry Onoda, "Personality Characteristics of High-Achieving and Under-Achieving Japanese-American Sanseis" (Ph.D. diss., Claremont Graduate School, 1974), 145–147.

27  Nakano, 231.

28  Mullins (1987), 325.

29  Mullins (1988), 218.

30  Ibid., 231.

(New York and Oxford: Oxford University Press, 1997), 18.

31  Nakano notes that in 1973, 88 percent of Sansei had completed some college training.

32  Kashima, 171, also states, "the modern Japanese American male has also taken on newer roles, removed from the authoritarian models of past generations."

33  Kashima, 60.

34  Jorge Aquino, "Dharma Bummed," in *San Francisco Weekly* 14, no. 47 (January, 1996):19, quoting Bishop Hakubun Watanabe. The Bishop is further quoted as saying that "he will promote efforts to attract the curious to Buddhism by using temples for popular Japanese cultural activities..."

35  Tuck, 223. Kashima, 152, says that reforms included Sunday Schools, women's associations, sermons and hymnals, primarily to placate Meiji authorities who favoured occidental ideas.

36  Buddhist priests participated in the World Parliament of Religions conference because they saw it as an opportunity to introduce Buddhism to the world and make it a "universal" religion. In James Ketelaar, *Of Heretics and Martyrs in Meiji Japan: Buddhism and Its Persecution* (Princeton: Princeton University Press, 1990), 138 and 171.

37  Tuck, 224.

38  Aquino, 16.

39  Kenneth Tanaka, "Issues of Ethnicity in the Buddhist Churches of America," in Williams and Queen, 10.

40  See Kenneth Tanaka, "A Prospectus of The Buddhist Churches of America: The Role of Ethnicity," *The Pure Land*, New Series no. 12 (December 1995): 126–130.

41  Mullins (1987), 327.

42  Rita Gross, "Buddhism and Feminism: Toward Their Mutual Transformation, Part 1" *The Eastern Buddhist* 19, no. 1 (Spring 1986): 44–45. Feminism also implies a position of advocacy.

43  Jiyu Kennett, quoted in Lenore Friedman, *Meetings with Remarkable Women: Buddhist Teachers in America* (Boston and London: Shambhala Publications, Inc., 2000), 197.

44  Catherine Wessinger, ed., *Religious Institutions and Women's Leadership: New Roles Inside the Mainstream* (Columbia, S.C.: University of South Carolina Press, 1996), 6.

45  Ibid., 7.

46   Paula Nesbitt, *Feminization of the Clergy in America: Occupational and Organizational Perspectives* (New York and Oxford: Oxford University Press, 1997), 18.

47   Ursula King, *Women and Spirituality: Voices of Protest and Promise* (London: Macmillan Education Ltd., 1989), 172.

48   Carolyn Klein, *Meeting the Great Bliss Queen: Buddhists, Feminists, and the Art of the Self.* (Boston: Beacon Press, 1995); Judith Simmer-Brown, *Dakini's Warm Breath: The Feminine Principle in Tibetan Buddhism.* (Boston and London: Shambhala Press, 2001); Anne Klein, "Finding a Self: Buddhist and Feminist Perspectives," in *Sharing New Vision: Gender and Values in American Culture*, ed. Clarissa W. Atkinson, Constance Buchanan and Josephine Miles (Ann Arbor, MI: UMI Research Press, 1987), 191–218.

49   Joanna Macy, *Mutual Causality in Buddhism and General Systems Theory: The Dharma of Natural Systems.* (Albany: State University of New York Press, 1991).

50   Rita Gross, *Buddhism After Patriarchy: A Feminist History, Analysis, and Reconstruction of Buddhism* (Albany: State University of New York Press, 1993), 19–22.

51   Until 2005, there were only three female ministers on the BCA active roster. The number more than doubled when newly-installed Bishop Koshin Ogui granted temple assignments to four more.

52   Lenore Friedman, *Meetings with Remarkable Women: Buddhist Teachers in America* (Boston and London: Shambhala Publications, Inc., 1987; revised and updated, 2000); Marianne Dresser, *Buddhist Women on the Edge: Contemporary Perspectives from the Western Frontier* (Berkeley: North Atlantic Books, 1996).

53   Ibid., 193.

54   Max Weber, *The Sociology of Religion* (Boston: Beacon Press, 1922), 104.

55   Nesbitt, 14.

56   Rick Fields, "Divided Dharma: White Buddhists, Ethnic Buddhists, and Racism" in *The Faces of Buddhism in America*, ed. Charles S. Prebish and Kenneth K. Tanaka (Berkeley, Los Angeles and London: University of California Press, 1998): 196 ff. The literature on American Buddhist women cited earlier refers to the "white," rather than ethnic Buddhist community.

57   It would also be useful to examine the Womanist movement, as well as Asian American Christian denominations, to compare their spiritual and

religious issues.

58  Edward C. Lehman, Jr., *Gender and Work: A Case for the Clergy* (Albany: State University of New York Press, 1993), 108.

59  Martha Long Ice, *Clergy Women and Their Worldviews: Calling for a New Age* (New York, Westport and London: Praeger Publishers, 1987), 45.

60  Ibid., 184.

61  Ibid.,198.

62  Lehman, 79–81. According to the maximalist view (of differences), "Masculine style involves the exercise of power over people, a concern for status and personal authority, excessive rationalism, approaching ethical dilemmas in a legalistic manner, and creating a protective distance between the minister and the congregation; while feminine style involves empowerment of the laity, downplaying clerical authority in favor of egalitarianism, a warm and approachable personal style, social activism, reliance on intuition, and the resolution of ethical dilemmas with concern for the well-being of all persons involved." Wessinger, 14, referring to Lehman's study.

63  Lehman, 192.

64  See Nesbitt, 17 and Wessinger, 7.

65  Karuna Dharma, quoted in Friedman, 235.

66  King, 79.

67  With thanks to Rev. Patti Nakai and Rev. Carol Himaka.

68  It should be noted that while Shinran praises the thirty-fifth vow in his writings, he also makes frequent allusion to the absence of form in the Pure Land.

69  Dobbins (1995), 121.

70  Ibid., 122.

71  Paul Harrison, "Who Gets to Ride in the Great Vehicle? Self-Image and Identity Among the Followers of Early Mahāyāna," *Journal of the International Association of Buddhist Studies* 10, no. 1 (1987): 79.

## NOTES TO CHAPTER THREE

1  Mary Daly, *The Church and the Second Sex* (New York: Harper and Row, 1968). 9.

2  See Appendix I.

3  See Appendix II.

4  According to Kenneth Tanaka, "A Prospectus of the Buddhist Churches of America: The Role of Ethnicity," *The Pure Land,* New Series, no. 12 (December 1995): 130, approximately twenty percent of Dharma School students are of mixed heritage.

5  It is possible that women represent a majority of active BCA members, but this is difficult to ascertain because membership statistics are not reported consistently by individual temples, and they are not registered on the basis whether the member is male or female, but rather by family and "head of family".

6  E-mail received November 6, 2003.

7  For example, see Harry Kitano, *Generations and Identity: The Japanese American* (Needham Heights, MA: Ginn, 1993). Even the all-encompassing Japanese American Citizens League (JACL) is grappling with plunging membership as young people "feel distanced from their cultural heritage" and wonder why the JACL is relevant to them today. See chapter five, youth responses regarding their ideal minister.

8  Kashima, 19.

9  Ibid., 40. Kashima later elucidates (p. 60), "The BCA retained the ideas of Buddhism as its core. The aim was to make Buddhism more acceptable, more understandable, more inclusive of all Buddhist thoughts, as well as less sectarian, less restrictive in membership, and more adaptable to the changing needs of the Nisei and Sansei. The Buddhists in America desired to lift, for the Nisei and their children, the veil of foreignness cast over their religion by the language and customs of the Issei."

10  This refers to the Buddhist philosophical meaning of the emptiness of "self."

11  Referring to Amida Buddha's vow to save all beings.

12  She is referring to some BCA versions of the *Three Treasures*.

13  For a detailed explanation, see Rita Gross, "Some Buddhist Perspectives on Goddess," in *Women and Goddess Traditions In Antiquity and Today*, ed. Karen L. King (Minneapolis: Fortress Press, 1997), 406–425.

14  This reference is not to a Shin Buddhist teaching, but the Buddhist story is widely recounted at BCA temples during the annual Urabon festival celebrated by Japanese Buddhists in memory of the deceased. See the

section on women in Chinese Buddhism in chapter one.

15  In fact, there are a number of female bodhisattvas. One of the most prominent is Kannon (Avalokiteśvara) who is often associated with Amida Buddha and is popular in Japan.

16  Eshinni was the wife of Shinran, whose extant letters reveal much about Shinran and his life. Kakushinni was their youngest daughter, credited with establishing the groundwork for what is now the Nishi Hongwanji institution. In 2002, delegates to the World Buddhist Women's Convention adopted a resolution that individual chapters annually celebrate an official "Kakushinni Day" to honour her.

17  Number in brackets refers to age, showing that age had no noticeable bearing on comments.

18  This may refer to the Head Abbot, who acquires his title through patrilineal inheritance; or to the fact that all of the positions of power in the sizable Hongwanji organization are occupied by men.

19  *Myokonin* (lit. "wonderfully excellent person") were humble Japanese laity who understood and lived in the Jōdo Shinshū teaching. There are a number of female exemplars, though ministers often cite famous male *myokonin* as examples.

20  *The Golden Chain* is a BCA verse encompassing the flavour of Shin Buddhism, that is regularly recited by Dharma School students.

21  Women were asked for their educational levels and professions on the survey. On the youth survey, respondents were asked for this information regarding their mothers.

22  *Komon* is roughly equivalent to an elder or senior advisor.

23  A Betsuin is an adaptation from the Japanese system. In the BCA, it is a large regional temple. Actually, at least two other Betsuin have female presidents.

24  For example, it is legendary in Japan that "salarymen" often hand over their paycheques to their wives, who are responsible for everything from household management and investments, to giving their husbands a modest daily stipend. However, observes Patricia Morley, *The Mountain is Moving: Japanese Women's Lives* (New York: New York University Press, 1999), 44–45, while women may control the family income, they generally take their status from their husband's position. The symbiotic relationship between husband and wife might also exist in America but the parameters would likely be different, and they would also change from generation to generation. Of course, this is not limited to the ethnic group in question.

25   E-mail received November 10, 2003.

26   E-mail received November 11, 2003.

27   This becomes evident in their response to the question of women in the ministry in chapter five.

28   Kenneth Tanaka, *Pure Land*, 127.

## NOTES TO CHAPTER FOUR

1   Based on the BCA 2004–2005 Directory.

2   See chapter five for comments on the ministry.

3   These are groups that may not be large enough to support their own temple but gather together regularly, often at a community center, to hear the dharma from a visiting minister. These days, they may also have some of the same activities and interest groups as a regular temple but on a much smaller scale.

4   See chapter two. Among Asian Americans, the outmarriage rate is highest for ethnic Japanese.

5   *Tokudo* is the initial ordination of a Shin Buddhist priest.

6   Fully ordained minister

7   Overseas minister

8   *Naikan* is a form of psychotherapy based on Jōdo Shinshū principles.

9   Annual dues to the BCA are assessed based on membership figures reported by the temple.

10   Irma Herrera, executive director of ERA, quoted by Joan Ryan, "Suddenly, S.F. Bursting with Pink: Women Taking Over Top Leadership Roles," *San Francisco Chronicle*, 23 January, 2004, sec. A, p. 17. The article is significant since BCA headquarters is in San Francisco and a large number of its temples are located in California. Could it escape notice that this is the kind of social environment in which members are immersed, and of which they could well be a part? It is reported that in San Francisco alone, the fire chief, the police chief, the district attorney, and the school superintendent are all women. In addition, the two state senators are women and another is the first U.S. House of Representatives minority leader in history. The chair and CEO of nearby Hewlett-Packard is also a woman.

11   *Toban* is a system in which pre-designated individuals or groups

take turns with duties.

12 Kenneth Tanaka, *Pure Land*, 131, estimates, "Even if we took the most optimistic figure ... two-thirds of the *sansei* who attended the temple in youth are no longer regular members or attendees of the temples."

13 This case will be addressed in the next chapter.

14 Rita Gross, *Buddhism After Patriarchy: A Feminist History, Analysis, and Reconstruction of Buddhism* (Albany: State University of New York Press, 1993), 35.

## NOTES TO CHAPTER FIVE

1 The reported response closely parallels the description of duties elaborated by Donald Tuck, *Buddhist Churches of America: Jodo Shinshū* (Lewiston and Queenston: The Edwin Mellen Press, 1987), 142–147, with the exception that he gives administration a more prominent role, preceding personal and social counsel.

2 I did not research attitudes regarding ministers' wives, or the opinions of ministers' wives, as this would be an entire topic of investigation in itself.

3 Tetsuden Kashima, *Buddhism in America: The Social Organization of an Ethnic Religious Institution* (Westport, Ct.: Greenwood Press, 1977),79. Also see Tuck, 81–93 and 155–156.

4 Significantly, on February 26, 2004, the Hongwanji Assembly passed an amendment to clause 26 of the Hongwanji Shuho (regulations). The clause formerly prescribed *bōmori* as the "wife of the *jūshoku* (resident minister)." The definition now reads, "a family member nominated by the *jūshoku*." The amendment removes not only discrimination based on sex but also on marital status, since the nominee may be either married or single. See also, "Bōmori – A Member of a Temple Family Nominated by the Resident Minister: A Man Can Become Bōmori," *Chugai Nippo* (Kyoto) on 27 January, 2004, p. 1. A *jūshoku* may be a man or a woman.

5 This means "wife" but at BCA temples, it is meant to be an honorific title given to the minister's wife.

6 Their comments are comparable to those of young Dori Takata, "Defining Membership," in *Pacific Citizen* 137, no. 4 (2003): 1, 2 and 9, who writes of declining new membership in the Japanese American Citizens League, "Embracing diversity within our community is key to increasing our

base of support, and attention to our language, actions, and subtle messages go hand-in-hand with thinking critically about how to be inclusive and open to change while holding on to our cultural identity. We need to make a conscious effort to make allies and supporters feel welcome, to solicit input and various points of view ..."

7 "Baggage Buddhism" or ethnic Buddhism refers to Jan Nattier's classification of the kind of Buddhism that was brought to America by Asian immigrants. Jan Nattier, "Who is a Buddhist? Charting the Landscape of Buddhist America," in *The Faces of Buddhism in America*, ed. Charles S. Prebish and Kenneth K. Tanaka (Berkeley, Los Angeles and London: University of California Press, 1998), 190.

8 Charles Prebish, *Luminous Passage: The Practice and Study of Buddhism in America* (Berkeley, Los Angeles and London: University of California Press, 1999), 264, quoting Lama Surya Das in a presentation at the Buddhism in America Conference, Boston, 17–19 January, 1997.

9 Tuck, 93–94.

10 Hongwanji Shiryō Kenkyūsho, ed., *Hongwanji shi*, vol. 3 (Jōdo Shinshū Hongwanji-ha Shūmusho, 1969), 655–656. In 1930, to prepare for the authorization of women ministers, special clauses were added to the regulations which specified that female ministers could not sit in the main altar area with male ministers; they could not be assigned as resident ministers; and they had no voting rights in the Hongwanji. However, in all other aspects, they had equal rights to a male minister. The regulations have since changed to allow greater equality. Significantly, due to the ground-breaking measure, a resolution for a movement to obtain civil rights for women in Japan was adopted at the November, 1930 meeting of the *fujinkai*. In 1931, a special department for female seminarians was established at Chuo Bukkyo Gakuin.

11 Information received by e-mail from Jōdo Shinshū Hongwanji-ha, International Department, September 12, 2003.

12 In 2004 it was announced that the Hongwanji Head Abbot's eldest daughter received *tokudo* ordination. This was the first occurrence of an Ohtani (the Abbot's surname) daughter doing so.

13 Information received by e-mail from Jōdo Shinshū Hongwanji-ha, International Department, September 12, 2003.

14 In my own experience, I have never encountered anything but a warm welcome, encouragement, gratitude, and respect from men and women of every age group. No doubt people are generally gracious, but what percentage truly oppose women in the ministry, and to what extent is

this based on experience rather than conjecture?

15  Paula Nesbitt, *Feminization of the Clergy in America*: Occupational and Organizational Perspectives (New York and Oxford: Oxford University Press, 1997), 4.

16  Masako Tanaka, "The Myth of Perfect Motherhood: Japanese Women's Dilemma," in *Speaking of Faith: Global Perspectives on Women, Religion and Social Change*, ed. Diana Eck and Devaki Jain (Philadelphia: New Society Publishers, 1987), 75–83.

17  See Jorge Aquino, "Dharma Bummed: The Buddhist Churches of America's Struggle to Keep the Faith," *SF Weekly* 14, no. 47 (January 3–9, 1996): 10–19.

18  Related to the BCA, the Institute of Buddhist Studies, located in Berkeley, California, is a graduate school for Shin Buddhist studies and a seminary for Shin ministerial education.  It is an affiliate of the Graduate Theological Union, a consortium of religious institutions representing various faith traditions. Thus, it offers broad contact with religious studies and issues in contemporary American society. Ministerial candidates who successfully complete the seminary program are qualified to take *tokudo* and *kyoshi* ordination training in Kyoto.

19  Larry Onoda, "Personality Characteristics of High-Achieving and Under-Achieving Japanese-American Sanseis" (Ph.D. diss., Claremont Graduate School, 1974), 142.

## NOTES TO CONCLUSION

1  The thirty-fifth vow of Dharmākara Bodhisattva, appearing in the main sutra of Jodo Shinshu, the *Sukhāvatī-vyūha Sūtra*, allows for women be transformed into men in order to attain Buddhahood. See chapter one.

# APPENDIX 1

## SURVEY OF WOMEN
## MEMBERS OF THE BCA

My name is Patricia Kanaya Usuki and I am a Master's degree candidate at the Graduate Theological Union and the Institute of Buddhist Studies. I invite you to participate in research I am undertaking for my thesis. I am examining the relationship between the teachings of Jōdo Shinshū and the perception of women in contemporary American Shin Buddhist institutions.

This survey will help me to get an idea of the views of women who are active in the Jōdo Shinshū sangha in America today. It is important because women's needs should be served in the best and most appropriate way possible, both now and in the future.

This is an anonymous survey. I do not wish to know your name or temple affiliation so you will not be put at risk of being personally identified with comments or other data. I plan to report on the information collected from this survey in my thesis. Some of it is statistical and other questions ask for brief comments, which I may or may not cite. If you do not wish a particular comment to be reported in my thesis, please write "do not cite" beside it. However, anything you do say will be very helpful to my research and hopefully to the future of Jōdo Shinshū in America.

Thank you very much for your co-operation and participation.

[Note: Numbers in brackets in questions one and two represent numbers of respondents.]

1.  Age group: 20+ (0)  30+ (8)  40+ (20)  50+ (39)  60+ (37)  70+ (55)  80+ (26)

2.  Issei (7)  Nisei (93)  Sansei (68)  Yonsei (2)  Other (including dual generation; Kibei) (15)

3.  First language: English—— Japanese—— Both the same——Other——

4. Educational level: Elementary School___ Middle School___ High School ___ Junior College or Equivalent ___ University undergraduate___Graduate School (specify degree)_____ Other (specify) _____

5. Occupations (past and present) _____
   _____
   _____

6. For how many years have you been participating in temple activities?___ years

7. What are your reasons for going to the temple? (Please number in order of reason)

   Religious___ Social ___Cultural ___Duty___ Children ___
   Other (specify) _____

8. Activities you attend or in which you participate or have participated:

   Regular religious services___ Study classes___ Dharma School (teacher) ___ Helping or leading child or youth activities ___ Temple administration ___ Newsletter ___ Board or committees ___ Temple maintenance___ Cooking ___ Fund raisers ___
   Clubs (specify)_____
   Other (specify) _____

9. Do you feel that women and men are perceived to be equal in the temple and in temple activities and duties? Yes___ No ___

   Please explain:_____
   _____
   _____
   _____

10. From your understanding of Buddhism and the Jōdo Shinshū teaching, do you feel that women and men are viewed equally in our doctrine?

    Yes___ No___

    Please give reasons: _____
    _____
    _____

11. What do you think some of the main duties of a minister are?

_____

_____

_____

12. Would you feel comfortable talking to a male minister about a personal issue? Yes___ No___

13. Would you feel comfortable talking to a female minister about a personal issue? Yes___ No___

14. In your opinion, are there positive aspects to having a female minister? (Specify) _____

_____

_____

_____

15. In your opinion, are there any drawbacks to having a female minister? (Specify) _____

_____

_____

_____

16. Should women be encouraged to become ministers? Yes___ No___
Reasons: _____

_____

_____

_____

17. Would you accept a woman as a minister at your temple/church?
Yes___ No___
Comments: _____

_____

_____

_____

18. Describe ways, if any, that women can serve and be served better by the BCA. _____

_____

_____

_____

# APPENDIX 2

## SURVEY OF THE JR. YOUNG BUDDHIST LEAGUE

My name is Patricia Kanaya Usuki and I am a Master's candidate at the Graduate Theological Union and the Institute of Buddhist Studies. I invite you to participate in research I am undertaking for my thesis. I am examining the relationship between the teachings of Shin Buddhism and the perception of women in contemporary American Shin Buddhist institutions.

This survey will help me to get an idea of the views of members of your age group. It is important because you are the future of Jōdo Shinshū in America and your needs should be served in the best and most appropriate way possible.

This is an anonymous survey. I do not wish to know your name or temple affiliation so you will not be put at risk of being personally identified with comments or other data. I plan to report on the information collected from this survey in my thesis. Some of it is statistical and other questions ask for brief comments, which I may or may not cite. If you do not want a comment to be reported in my thesis, please write "do not cite" beside it. However, any informative comments you do make will be very helpful to my research and hopefully to the future of Jōdo Shinshū in America.

Thank you for your co-operation. Please return this survey to your advisor when completed.

[Note: Numbers in brackets in questions one and two represent numbers of respondents.]

1. Female (81)   Male (80)

2. Age___

3. Issei (2)   Nisei (13)   Sansei (20)   Yonsei (103)   Other (incl. dual generation) (23)

4. After graduating from high school, what are your immediate plans?

Attend college or other educational institution____Work full time____
Other (specify)_____

5. Do you plan to have a career some day? Yes____ No____
   Please specify

6. What level of education does your mother have?
   ____ High school
   ____ Junior college or equivalent
   ____ Bachelor's degree
   ____ Graduate school (specify degree )_____
   ____ Other (specify )_____

7. Does your mother work? Yes____ No____ (If "yes," what does she do?
   _____

8. For how many years have you been participating in temple activities?
   years____

9. Who influenced your religious life most?
   Mother____ Father____ Both____ Other (specify)_____

10. What are your reasons for going to the temple? (Please number in
    order of reason)
    Religious____ Social____
    Sports____ Cultural____
    Parents____ Other (specify)_____

11. Do you feel that men and women are treated equally in the temple
    and in temple activities and duties? Yes____ No____ (If you answered
    "no," please explain):_____
    _____
    _____
    _____

12. From your understanding of Buddhism and the Jōdo Shinshū teach-
    ing, do you feel that women and men are viewed equally in our doctrine?
    Yes____ No____

    (Please give reasons)_____
    _____

_____
_____
_____

13. Would you consider becoming a Jōdo Shinshū minister?

    Yes___ No___

14. Why or why not?_____
    _____
    _____
    _____

15. What do you think some of the main duties of a minister are?
    _____
    _____
    _____
    _____

16. Would you feel comfortable talking to a male minister about a personal issue?

    Yes___ No___

17. Would you feel comfortable talking to a female minister about a personal issue?

    Yes___ No___

18. Should women be encouraged to become ministers?

    Yes___ No___

    Reasons: _____
    _____
    _____
    _____

# APPENDIX 3

## TOPOLOGY OF
## LAYWOMEN INTERVIEWED

I.   Ethnic Japanese

Age Range:    40+ (1)

50+ (3)

60+ (3)

70  (1)

Generation:   Nisei  (4)

Sansei (4)

II.  Four non-ethnic Japanese women with *tokudo* ordination were also interviewed.

# BIBLIOGRAPHY

Bancroft, Anne. "Women in Buddhism." In *Women in the World's Religions, Past and Present,* ed. Ursula King, 81–104. New York: Paragon House, 1987.

Barnes, Nancy Schuster. "Buddhism." In *Women In World Religions*, ed. Arvind Sharma, 105–133. Albany: State University of New York Press, 1987.

Becker, Carl. "Japanese Pure Land Buddhism in Christian America." *Buddhist-Christian Studies* 10 (1990): 143–156.

Bernhardt, Kathryn. *Women and Property in China, 960–1949*. Stanford: Stanford University Press, 1999.

Birge, Bettine. *Women, Property, and Confucian Reaction in Sung and Yuan China (960–1368)*. Cambridge: Cambridge University Press, 2002.

Blackstone, Kathryn R. *Women in the Footsteps of the Buddha: Struggle for Liberation in the Therigatha*. Surrey, U.K.: Curzon Press, 1998.

Bloom, Alfred. "The Western Pure Land." *Tricycle: The Buddhist Review* 4, no. 4 (1995): 58–63.

————. "The Unfolding of the Lotus: A Survey of Recent Developments in Shin Buddhism in the West." *Buddhist-Christian Studies* 10 (1990): 157–164.

Bonacich, Edna and John Modell. *The Economic Basis of Ethnic Solidarity: Small Business in the Japanese American Community*. Berkeley, Los Angeles and London: University of California Press, 1980.

Boucher, Sandy. *Opening the Lotus: A Woman's Guide to Buddhism*. Boston: Beacon Press, 1997.

————. *Turning the Wheel: American Women Creating the New Buddhism*. Boston: Beacon Press, 1993 (updated).

Buddhist Churches of America, *Buddhist Churches of America, 2003–*

*2004 Directory.* San Francisco: Buddhist Churches of America, 2003.

_____. *Buddhist Churches of America: 2002 Annual Report.* San Francisco: Buddhist Churches of America, 2003.

_____. *Buddhist Churches of America: A Legacy of the First Hundred Years.* San Francisco: Buddhist Churches of America, 1998.

Cabezon, Jose Ignacio. "Mother Wisdom, Father Love: Gender-based Imagery in Mahāyāna Buddhist Thought." In *Buddhism, Sexuality and Gender*, ed Jose Ignacio Cabezon, 181–199. Albany: State University of New York Press, 1985.

Chakravarty, Uma. *The Social Dimensions of Early Buddhism.* Delhi: Oxford University Press, 1987.

_____. "The Social Philosophy of Buddhism and the Problem of Inequality." *Social Compass* 33, no. 2–3 (1986): 199–221.

Chung, Priscilla Ching. "Power and Prestige: Palace Women in the Northern Sung (960–1126)." In *Women in China: Current Directions in Historical Scholarship*, ed. Richard W. Guisso and Stanley Johannesen, 99–112. Youngstown, N.Y.: Philo Press, 1981.

Cole, Alan. *Mothers and Sons in Chinese Buddhism.* Stanford: Stanford University Press, 1998.

Daly, Mary. *The Church and the Second Sex.* New York: Harper and Row, 1968.

Darian, Jean. "Social and Economic Factors in the Rise of Buddhism." *Sociological Analysis* 38, no. 3 (1977): 226–238.

De Silva, Sharma. The Place of Women In Buddhism. Paper presented to the Midlands Buddhist Society (UK), November 1988, current edition June 1994; available from http://www.enabling.org/ia/vipassana/Archive/D/DeSilva/WomenInBuddhism/womenInBuddhismSwarnaDeSilva.html; Internet; accessed 17 October 2002.

Dobbins, James. *Jōdo Shinshū: Shin Buddhism in Medieval Japan.* Bloomington and Indianapolis: Indiana University Press, 1989.

_____. "Women's Birth in the Pure Land as Women: Intimations from the Letters of Eshinni." *The Eastern Buddhist* 28, no. 1 (1995): 108–122.

Dresser, Marianne, ed. *Buddhist Women on the Edge: Contemporary*

*Perspectives from the Western Frontier.* Berkeley: North Atlantic Books, 1996.

Ducor, Jerome. "The Canon Laws of Honganji and Doctrinal Authority." *The Pure Land,* New Series, no. 12 (December 1995): 142–151.

Ebrey, Patricia Buckley. *The Inner Quarters: Marriage and Lives of Chinese Women in the Sung Period.* Berkeley: University of California Press, 1993.

————. "Women in the Kinship System of the Southern Song Upper Class." In *Women in China: Current Directions in Historical Scholarship,* ed. Richard W. Guisso and Stanley Johannesen, 113–128. Youngstown, N.Y.: Philo Press, 1981.

Eck, Diana L. and Devaki Jain, eds. *Speaking of Faith: Global Perspectives on Women, Religion and Social Change.* Philadelphia: New Society Publishers, 1987.

Falk, Nancy A. "The Case of the Vanishing Nuns: The Fruits of Ambivalence in Ancient Indian Buddhism." In *Unspoken Worlds: Women's Religious Lives in Non-Western Cultures,* ed. Nancy A. Falk and Rita M. Gross, 207–224. San Francisco: Harper and Row, 1979.

Faure, Bernard. *The Power of Denial: Buddhism, Purity, and Gender.* Princeton: Princeton University Press, 2003.

Feagan, Joe R., and Nancy Fujitaki. "On the Assimilation of Japanese Americans." *Amerasia Journal* 1, no.4 (February 1972): 13–31.

Fernandez, Audrey McK., "Women in Buddhism: For 2500 Years, A Persisting Force." In *Spring Wind: Buddhist Cultural Forum* 6, no. 1, 2, and 3 (1986): 35–57.

Findly, Ellison, ed. *Women's Buddhism, Buddhism's Women: Tradition, Revision, Renewal.* Boston: Wisdom Publications, 2000.

Foulk, T. Griffith. "Myth, Ritual, and Monastic Practice." In *Religion and Society in T'ang and Sung China,* ed. Patricia Ebrey and Peter Gregory, 147–208. Honolulu: University of Hawaii Press, 1993.

Friedman, Lenore. *Meetings with Remarkable Women: Buddhist Teachers in America.* Boston and London: Shambhala Publications, 1987. Revised and updated, 2000.

Friedman, Lenore and Susan Moon, eds. *Being Bodies: Buddhist Women on the Paradox of Enlightenment.* Boston and London: Shambhala Publications, 1997.

Fujieda, Mioko. "Japan's First Phase of Feminism." In *Japanese Women: New Feminist Perspectives on the Past, Present, and Future*, ed. Kumiko Fujimura-Fanselow and Atsuko Kameda, 323–342. New York: The Feminist Press at The City University of New York, 1995.

Fujimura-Fanselow, Kumiko and Atsuko Kameda, ed. *Japanese Women: New Feminist Perspectives on the Past, Present, and Future*. New York: The Feminist Press at The City University of New York, 1995.

Fugita, Stephen S. and David J. O'Brien. *Japanese-American Ethnicity: The Persistence of Community*. Seattle and London: University of Washington Press, 1991.

Gombrich, Richard. *Theravāda Buddhism: A Social History from Ancient Benares to Modern Columbo*. London: Routledge and Kegan Paul, 1988.

Gross, Rita. *Soaring and Settling: Buddhist Perspectives on Contemporary Social and Religious Issues*. New York: Continuum, 1998.

————. "Some Buddhist Perspectives on the Goddess." In *Women and Goddess Traditions*, ed. Karen L. King, 406–425. Minneapolis: Fortress Press, 1997.

————. *Feminism and Religion: An Introduction*. Boston: Beacon Press, 1996.

————. *Buddhism After Patriarchy: A Feminist History, Analysis, and Reconstruction of Buddhism*. Albany: State University of New York Press, 1993.

————. "Buddhism and Feminism: Toward Their Mutual Transformation, Part 1." *The Eastern Buddhist* 19, no. 1 (Spring 1986): 44–58.

Haddad, Yvonne Yazbeck, and Ellison Banks Findly, eds. *Women, Religion and Social Change*. Albany: State University of New York Press, 1985.

Harrison, Paul. "Women in the Pure Land: Some Reflections on the Textual Sources." *Journal of Indian Philosophy* 26, no. 6 (1998): 553–572.

————. "Who Gets to Ride in the Great Vehicle? Self-Image and Identity Among the Followers of Early Mahāyāna." *Journal of the International Association of Buddhist Studies* 10, no. 1 (1987): 67–89.

Hecker, Hellmuth. *Buddhist Women at the Time of the Buddha*. Sri Lanka:

Buddhist Publication Society, 1982.

Heirman, Ann. "Chinese Nuns and their Ordination in Fifth Century China." *Journal of the International Association of Buddhist Studies* 24, no. 2 (2001): 275–304.

Hirakawa, Akira. "The History of Buddhist Nuns in Japan." Translated by Karma Lekshe Tsomo. *Buddhist-Christian Studies* 12 (1992): 147–158.

Hirota, Dennis, Hisao Inagaki, Michio Tokunaga and Ryushin Uryuzu, trans. *The Collected Works of Shinran*, Vol. 1 & 2. Kyoto: Jodo Shinshu Hongwanji-ha, 1997.

Hongwanji International Center. *Jodo Shinshu: A Guide*. Kyoto: Hongwanji Shuppansha, 2002.

Hongwanji Shiryō Kenkyūsho, ed. *Hongwanji shi*, Vol. 3. Kyoto: Jōdo Shinshū Hongwanji-ha Shūmusho, 1969.

Horinouchi, Isao. "Americanized Buddhism: A Sociological Analysis of a Protestantized Japanese Religion." Ph.D. dissertation, University of California, Davis, 1973.

Horner, Isaline B. *Women Under Primitive Buddhism: Laywomen and Almswomen*. London: Routledge and Kegan Paul Ltd., 1930. Reprint, Delhi: Motilal Barnasidass, 1975.

Hsieh, Ding-hwa E. "Images of Women in Ch'an Buddhist Literature of the Sung Period." In *Buddhism in the Sung*, ed. Peter N. Gregory and Daniel Al Getz, 148–187. Honolulu: University of Hawaii Press, 1999.

Ice, Martha Long. *Clergy Women and Their Worldviews: Calling for a New Age*. New York, Westport and London: Praeger Publishers, 1987.

Ichioka, Yuji. "*Amerika Nadeshiko*: Japanese Immigrant Women in the United States, 1900–1924." In *American Immigration and Ethnicity*, vol. 12, *Ethnicity and Gender: The Immigrant Woman*, ed. George E. Pozzetta, 97–115. New York and London: Garland Publishing Inc., 1991.

Ito, Robert. "The Twenty-five Most Noteworthy Asians in America in 2001." *aMagazine* (December 2001–January 2002): 48–61.

Inagaki, Hisao. *The Three Pure Land Sutras*, 2d ed. Kyoto: Nagata Bunshodo, 1995.

Jon, Ho-Ryeon. "Can Women Achieve Enlightenment? A Critique of Sexual Transformation for Enlightenment." In *Buddhist Women Across Cultures*, ed. Karma Leshe Tsomo, 123–141. Albany: State University of New York Press, 1999.

Kashima, Tetsuden. *Buddhism in America: The Social Organization of an Ethnic Religious Institution*. Westport, Ct.: Greenwood Press, 1977.

———. "The Buddhist Churches of America: Challenges for Change in the 21st Century." *Pacific World: Journal of the Institute of Buddhist Studies* 6 (Fall 1990): 28–40.

Ketelaar, James Edward. *Of Heretics and Martyrs in Meiji Japan: Buddhism and Its Persecution*. Princeton: Princeton University Press, 1990.

King, Karen L., ed. *Women and Goddess Traditions in Antiquity and Today*. Minneapolis: Fortress Press, 1997.

King, Sallie B. "Egalitarian Philosophies in Sexist Institutions: The Life of Satomi-san, Shinto Miko and Zen Buddhist Nun." *Journal of Feminist Studies in Religion* 4, no.1 (Spring 1988): 7–26.

King, Ursula. *Women and Spirituality: Voices of Protest and Promise*. London: Macmillan Education Ltd., 1989.

King, Ursula, ed. *Religion and Gender*. Oxford: Blackwell, 1995.

———. *Women in the World's Religions, Past and Present*. New York: Paragon House, 1987.

Kitano, Harry L. *Generations and Identity: The Japanese American*. Needham Heights, MA: Ginn, 1993.

Klein, Anne C. "Finding a Self: Buddhist and Feminist Perspectives." In *Sharing New Vision: Gender and Values in American Culture*, ed. Clarissa W. Atkinson, Constance Buchanan and Josephine Miles, 191–218. Ann Arbor, MI: UMI Research Press, 1987.

Klein, Carolyn Anne. *Meeting the Great Bliss Queen: Buddhists, Feminists, and the Art of the Self*. Boston: Beacon Press, 1995.

Knapp, Bettina L. *Images of Japanese Women: A Westerner's View*. Troy, N.Y.: The Whitston Publishing Co., 1992.

Kujo, Takeko. *Muyuge: Flower Without Sorrow*. Los Angeles: The Nembutsu Press, 1985.

Kusuma, Bhikkhuni. "Inaccuracies in Buddhist Women's History." In *Innovative Buddhist Women: Swimming Against the Stream*, ed. Karma Lekshe Tsomo, 5–12. Surrey, U.K.: Curzon, 2000.

Layman, Emma. *Buddhism in America*. Chicago: Nelson-Hall Inc., 1976.

Lee, Essie E. *Nurturing Success: Successful Women of Color and Their Daughters*. Westport, CT and London: Praeger Publishers, 2000.

Lee, Lily Xiao Hong, *The Virtue of Yin: Studies on Chinese Women*. Sydney: Wild Peony Pty. Ltd., 1994.

Lehman, Edward C., Jr. *Gender and Work: A Case for the Clergy*. Albany: State University of New York Press, 1993.

Levering, Miriam. "Miao-Tao and Her Teacher Ta-hui." In *Buddhism in the Sung,* ed. Peter N. Gregory and Daniel A. Getz, 188–219. Honolulu: University of Hawaii Press, 1999.

_____. "Dogen's *Raihaitokuzui* and Women Teaching in Sung Ch'an." *The Journal of the International Association of Buddhist Studies* 21, no. 1 (1998): 77–110.

_____. "Stories of Enlightened Women in Ch'an and the Chinese Buddhist Female Bodhisattva/Goddess Tradition." In *Women in Goddess Traditions in Antiquity and Today*, ed. Karen L. King, 137–176. Minneapolis: Fortress Press, 1997.

_____. "Lin-chi (Rinzai) Ch'an and Gender: The Rhetoric of Equality and the Rhetoric of Heroism." In *Buddhism, Sexuality, and Gender*, ed. Jose Ignacio Cabezon, 137–156. Albany: State University of New York Press, 1985.

_____. "The Dragon Girl and the Abbess of Mo-Shan: Gender and Status in the Ch'an Buddhist Tradition." *Journal of the International Association of Buddhist Studies* 5, no. 1 (1982): 19–35.

Macy, Joanna. *Mutual Causality in Buddhism and General Systems Theory: The Dharma of Natural Systems*. Albany: State University of New York Press, 1991.

Matsunaga, Daigan and Alicia Matsunaga. *Foundation of Japanese Buddhism,* Vol. 1 & 2. Los Angeles and Tokyo: Buddhist Books International, 1974.

McLellan, Janet. *Many Petals of the Lotus: Five Asian Buddhist Communities in Toronto*. Toronto: University of Toronto Press, Inc., 1999.

Minamoto, Junko."Buddhism and the Historical Construction of Sexuality in Japan." *U.S.-Japan Women's Journal* Vol. 5, 1993.

_____. "Buddhist Attitudes: A Woman's Perspective." In *Women, Religion and Sexuality: Studies on the Impact of Religious Teachings on Women*, ed. Jeanne Becher, 154–171. Geneva: WCC Publications, 1990.

Morley, Patricia. *The Mountain is Moving: Japanese Women's Lives*. New York: New York University Press, 1999.

Montero, Darrel. *Japanese Americans: Changing Patterns of Ethnic Affiliation Over Three Generations*. Boulder, CO: Westview Press, 1980.

Mullins, Mark. "The Organizational Dilemmas of Ethnic Churches: A Case Study of Japanese Buddhism in Canada." *Sociological Analysis* 49, no. 3 (1988): 217–233.

_____. "The Life-Cycle of Ethnic Churches in Sociological Perspective." *Japanese Journal of Religious Studies* 14, no. 4 (1987): 321–334.

Murcott, Susan. *The First Buddhist Women: Translation and Commentaries on the Therigatha*. Berkeley: Parallax Press, 1991.

Nakano, Mei. *Japanese American Women: Three Generations 1890–1990*. Berkeley and Sebastopol: Mina Press Publishing, 1990.

Nattier, Jan. "Visible and Invisible." *Tricycle: The Buddhist Review* 5, no. 1 (1995): 42–49.

Nesbitt, Paula. *Feminization of the Clergy of America: Occupational and Organizational Perspectives*. New York and Oxford: Oxford University Press, 1997.

Nishimura, Hiro. *Trials and Triumphs of the Nikkei*. Mercer Island, WA: Fukuda Publishers, 1993.

Obeyesekere, Ranjini. *Portraits of Buddhist Women: Stories from the Saddharmaratnāvliya*. Albany: State University of New York, 2001.

Ohtani, Yoshiko. *The Life of Eshinni: Wife of Shinran Shonin*. Kyoto: Jōdo Shinshū Hongwanji-ha, 1990.

Okano, Haruko. "Women's Image and Place in Japanese Buddhism." In *Japanese Women: New Feminist Perspectives on the Past, Present, and Future*, ed. Kumiko Fujimura-Fanselow and Atsuko Kameda, 15–28. New York: The Feminist Press at The City University of New York, 1995.

Onoda, Larry. "Personality Characteristics of High-Achieving and Under-

Achieving Japanese-American Sanseis." Ph.D. diss., Claremont Graduate School, 1974.

Paul, Diana. *The Buddhist Feminine Ideal: Queen Śrīmālā and the Tathāgatagarbha*. Missoula, MT: Scholars Press, 1980.

_____. *Women in Buddhism: Images of the Feminine in Mahāyāna Tradition*. Berkeley: Asian Humanities Press, 1979. Reprinted Berkeley: University of California Press, 1985.

Pierce, Lori. "Diversity as Practice: Thinking about Race and 'American' Buddhism." In *Innovative Buddhist Women: Swimming Against the Stream*, ed. Karma Lekshe Tsomo, 277–284. Richmond, Surrey: Curzon Press, 2000.

Prebish, Charles S. *Luminous Passage: The Practice and Study of Buddhism in America*. Berkeley: University of California Press, 1999.

Prebish, Charles S. and Martin Baumann, eds. *Westward Dharma: Buddhism Beyond Asia*. Berkeley: University of California Press, 2002.

Prebish, Charles S. and Kenneth K. Tanaka, eds. *The Faces of Buddhism in America*. Berkeley: University of California Press, 1998.

Rogers, Minor L. and Ann T. Rogers. *Rennyo: The Second Founder of Shin Buddhism*. Berkeley: Asian Humanities Press, 1991.

Ruether, Rosemary Radford and Rosemary Skinner Keller, eds. *Women and Religion in America, Volume 3: 1900–1968 A Documentary Perspective*. San Francisco: Harper and Row, 1986.

Sangharakshita. *The Eternal Legacy: An Introduction to the Canonical Literature of Buddhism*. London: Tharpa Publications, 1985.

Sangren, P. Steven. "Female Gender in Chinese Religious Symbols: Kuan Yin, Ma Tsu, and the Eternal Mother." *Signs* 9, no. 1 (1983): 4–25.

Schopen, Gregory. *Bones, Stones, and Buddhist Monks: Collected Papers on the Archaeology, Epigraphy, and Texts of Monastic Buddhism in India*. Honolulu: University of Hawaii Press, 1997.

Schuster, Nancy. "Striking a Balance: Women and Images of Women in Early Chinese Buddhism." In *Women, Religion and Social Change*, ed. Yvonne Yazbeck Haddad and Ellison Banks Findly, 87–112. Albany: State University of New York Press, 1985.

_____. "Changing the Female Body: Wise Women and the Bodhisattva

Career in Some *Mahāratnakūtasūtras*." *The Journal of the International Association of Buddhist Studies* 4, no. 1 (1981): 24–69.

Seager, Richard Hughes. *The World's Parliament of Religions: The East/ West Encounter, Chicago, 1893*. Bloomington: Indiana University Press, 1995.

_____. *Buddhism in America*. New York: Columbia University Press, 1999.

Sharma, Arvind. "How and Why Did Women in Ancient India Become Buddhist Nuns?" *Sociological Analysis* 38, no.3 (1977): 239–251.

Sidor, Ellen S., ed. *A Gathering of Spirit: Women Teaching in American Buddhism*. Cumberland, R.I.: Primary Point Press, 1987.

Simmer-Brown, Judith. *Dakini's Warm Breath: The Feminine Principle in Tibetan Buddhism*. Boston and London: Shambhala, 2001.

_____. "The Roar of the Lioness: Women's Dharma in the West." In *Westward Dharma: Buddhism Beyond Asia*, ed. Charles Prebish and Martin Baumann, 309–323. Berkeley: University of California Press, 2002.

Sponberg, Alan. "Attitudes Toward Women and the Feminine in Early Buddhism." In *Buddhism, Sexuality and Gender*, ed. Jose Ignacio Cabezon, 3–36. Albany: State University of New York Press, 1992.

Takemi, Momoko. "Menstruation Sutra Belief in Japan." *Japanese Journal of Religious Studies* 10 (June–September, 1983): 229–246.

Talim, Meena. *Women in Early Buddhist Literature*. Bombay: University of Bombay Press, 1972.

Tanaka, Kenneth. "A Prospectus of the Buddhist Churches of America: The Role of Ethnicity." *The Pure Land*, New Series, no. 12 (December 1995): 121–141.

Tanaka, Masako. "The Myth of Perfect Motherhood: Japanese Women's Dilemma." In *Speaking of Faith: Global Perspectives on Women, Religion and Social Change*, ed. Diana Eck and Devaki Jain, 75–83. Philadelphia: New Society Publishers, 1987.

Teiser, Stephen. "The Growth of Purgatory." In *Religion and Society in T'ang and Sung China*, ed. Patricia Ebrey and Peter Gregory, 115–145. Honolulu: University of Hawaii Press, 1993.

Thurman, Robert A.F., trans. *The Holy Teaching of Vimalakīrti*. University Park: Pennsylvania State University Press, 1987.

Toji, Dean. "The Rise of a Nikkei Generation." In *New Face of Asian Pacific America: Numbers, Diversity and Change in the Twenty-first Century*, ed. Dennis Arguelles and Eric Yo Ping Lai, 73–78. San Francisco: Asian Week with UCLA Asian American Studies Center Press, 2003.

Tsai, Kathryn. "The Chinese Buddhist Monastic Order for Women: The First Two Centuries." In *Women In China: Current Directions in Historical Scholarship*, ed. Richard W. Guisso and Stanley Johannesen, 1–20. Youngstown, N.Y.: Philo Press, 1981.

Tsomo, Karma Lekshe, ed. *Innovative Buddhist Women: Swimming Against the Stream*. Richmond, Surrey: Curzon Press, 2000.

_____. *Buddhist Women Across Cultures: Realizations*. Albany: State University of New York Press, 1999.

_____. *Buddhism Through American Women's Eyes*. Ithaca: Snow Lion Publications, 1995.

Tuck, Donald R. *Buddhist Churches of America: J do Shinsh* . Lewiston, N.Y. and Queenston, Ont.: The Edwin Mellen Press, 1987.

Uchino, Kumiko. "The Status Elevation Process of Soto Sect Nuns in Modern Japan." In *Speaking of Faith: Global Perspectives on Women, Religion and Social Change,* ed. Diana Eck and Devaki Jain, 159–173. Philadelphia: New Society Publishers, 1987.

Ueki, Masatoshi. *Gender Equality in Buddhism*. New York: Peter Lang Publishing, Inc., 2001.

Unno, Tetsuo. "Notes on the Americanization of J do Shinsh Buddhism: Urgency, Adaptation, and Existential Relevance in America, 1986 and Beyond." *Pacific World*, New Series, no. 2 (Fall 1986): 11–17.

Victoria, Brian. *Zen at War.* New York and Tokyo: Weatherhill, 1997.

Walker, Caroline Bynum, Steven Harrell and Paula Richman, ed. *Gender and Religion: On the Complexity of Symbols*. Boston: Beacon Press, 1986.

Walters, Jonathan S. "A Voice from the Silence: The Buddha's Mother's Story." In *History of Religions* (Chicago) 33, no. 4 (1994): 358–379.

Warner, Stephen R. and Judith G. Wittner. *Gatherings in Diaspora: Religious Communities and the New Immigration*. Philadelphia: Temple University Press, 1998.

Wayman, Alex and Hideko Wayman, trans. *The Lion's Roar of Queen r m l : A Buddhist Scripture on the Tath gatagarbha Theory*. New

York and London: Columbia University Press, 1974.

Weber, Max. *The Sociology of Religion,* 4th ed. Translated by Ephraim Fischoff with a foreword by Ann Swidler. Boston: Beacon Press, 1993.

Wessinger, Catherine, ed. *Religious Institutions and Women's Leadership: New Roles Inside the Mainstream.* Columbia, S.C.: University of South Carolina Press, 1996.

Williams, Duncan Ryuken and Christopher S. Queen, ed. *American Buddhism: Methods and Findings in Recent Scholarship.* Surrey: Curzon Press, 1999.

Willis, Janice. "Nuns and Benefactresses: The Role of Women in the Development of Buddhism." In *Women, Religion and Social Change,* ed. Yvonne Yazbeck Haddad and Ellison Banks Findly, 59–85. Albany: State University of New York Press, 1985.

Wilson, Liz. *Charming Cadavers: Horrific Figurations of the Feminine in Indian Buddhist Hagiographic Literature.* Chicago: University of Chicago Press, 1996.

Yü, Chün-fang. *Kuan-yin: The Chinese Transformation of Avalokiteśvara.* New York: Columbia University Press, 2001.

Zen Lotus Society, ed. *Women and Buddhism*: *A Special Issue of Spring Wind–Buddhist Cultural Forum* 6, no. 1, 2 and 3. Toronto and Ann Arbor, 1986.

Zikmund, Barbara Brown, Adair T. Lummis and Patricia M.Y. Chang, eds. *Clergy Women: An Uphill Calling.* Louisville, KY: Westminster John Knox Press, 1998.

# ABOUT THE BEC

The Orange County Buddhist Church Buddhist Education Center (BEC), is the Buddhist educational program of the Orange County Buddhist Church, located in Anaheim, California. The BEC offers a variety of classes and seminars on Buddhism and Jōdo Shinshū in three eight week long sessions in the fall, winter, and spring. Courses range from Introduction to Buddhism and Jodo Shinshu, to textual study of Shin texts like the Larger Sutra and the Shoshinge, to related courses like Zen and Shin Buddhism, Buddhist Views of Life and Death, and Buddhist Calligraphy.

In addition to the educational program, the BEC also publishes books on Shin Buddhism. Our first publication was "Coffinman: The Journal of a Buddhist Mortician,"by Shinmon Aoki, which is a fascinating story of how one man came to meet the Shin Buddhist teachings through his work as a mortician, and how he came to sense immeasurable light in all things.

Future publications forthcoming are a translation of a work by Hideo Yonezawa on Shin Buddhism, a reprint of the book "The Hands and Feet of the Heart", the story of Hisako Nakamura, and a translation of the Buddhist comic book on the life of Genza the Myokonin.

Please visit our website at: www.bca-ocbc.org for information on our BEC program, Buddhist messages on our website, and notification of future publications.